Making
the
Grade

A Practical Guide for
Grading and Evaluating
Homeschooled Children

by Lesha Myers MA.Ed.

www.Cameron-Publishing.com

ISBN 978-0-9794506-1-7

Cover pictures: Top and bottom left by Lesha Myers. Right by Kathy Winship. Back cover by Brad Human, Brad Human Photography.

Printed in the United States of America

10 9   8   7   6   5   4   3

For more information go to www.Cameron-Publishing.com

To Bethany Bennett,
who taught me how to make the grade.

Thank You!

I would like to thank the mentor moms of Cameron Academy for sharing their expertise and allowing themselves to be interviewed for the "How We Made the Grade" sidebars of this book.

Cameron Academy is a private Christian school, an independent study program, designed to support, equip, hold accountable, and encourage parents in their God-given calling to give their children a Christ-centered education at home.

As part of this process, each Cameron member is assigned a mentor mom, an experienced homeschooler who has exhibited a love of the Lord and a desire to serve others. The wisdom and insight these women shared has helped to put a personal face on the issue of grading. I'd like to thank these busy moms who gave their time to this project:

❧ Joni Carlson

❧ Susan Grunder

❧ Sandra Lundin

❧ Diane Schachterle

❧ Amy Turner

❧ Sarah Young

All of these moms have been homeschooling for at least five years. Some have large families, while others have small. Some have young children, while others have home school, high school graduates. Some have all boys, some all girls, and some are blessed with both. They are a great group to work with and constantly bless and encourage me.

To allow the mentor moms to be open and forthright, while at the same time protecting their children's privacy, I have not identified the author of each comment. With one or two exceptions, all of the sidebar comments are excerpts from interviews with these women.

Table of Contents

Part One
Setting the Stage

*Containing foundational information applicable to the
subject of grading and evaluation as a whole.*

Chapter 1
What is Grading Anyway?

If any topic generates controversy among homeschool parents, it is grading. From a somewhat rebellious, "Why do I have to do this anyway?" to a despairing, "I can't do this! I don't even know how!" the task of evaluating our own children produces a strong emotional response.

Beneath the wide range of reactions lurks a common feeling: inadequacy. How do parents evaluate their own children? Classroom grading models do not always apply to the homeschool, and we throw up our hands in despair. What an impossible task, we think. No, not impossible. We just need some tools.

This book contains tools. It offers many practical methods you can use to honestly and ethically grade and evaluate your own children.

❧Whom should we grade?

Lower Elementary Students? No!

Before we begin, we need to decide whom to grade. It has been my pleasure to know several dedicated moms beginning their homeschool adventure with children in kindergarten. Wanting to do everything "right," these moms push themselves and their children far beyond what is needed. I want to be very clear: grading is *not* for you! In fact, formal grading should not begin until your child's upper elementary years. Although it is hard to be precise since children mature at different rates, I believe most children benefit from formal evaluation only in later grades.

Young children spend most of their time learning skills rather than content. They attach a sound to a letter, then blend these sounds to read. They associate a numeric value with a symbol, then combine these with other symbols to add. Children conquer these skills at different times. Should they receive a poor grade because they do not march to another's timetable? Emphatically, no!

Some children learn to read effortlessly at the age of three. Not mine. My children worked hard. While others were whizzing through Plato in second grade (or so I thought at the time) we were stuck on McGuffey's Primer. Now, however, they all read just fine—some, in fact, better than their mother.

Of what value would it have been to set a goal of reading through a particular book or mastering a number of phonograms, only to have my children fall short and receive a grade of C, D, or even (horrors!) an F? No, we

---

A Mentor Mom Shares
HOW WE MADE THE GRADE

"I didn't see much benefit in making my children grade conscious while they were in the primary grades. My oldest was in second grade when I brought her home and started homeschooling. At that early age I was concerned about mastering basic skills, so those were the only areas in which I kept some kind of running tab on her progress.

"We explored other areas for fun. We were learning, but it was exposure; it was not mastery. We read together, went on field trips and learned about the police station, without feeling the need to come home and write a report every time.

"I think my attitude reflected a little rebellion. Before my children were born I taught junior high and high school. I had no problem having to grade my students, but I wanted to bring my daughter home and relax, in the sense of letting loose some of those traditional school shackles and regulations. And for me, trying to find my way, making sure I wasn't bringing school home and making my homeschool look like the traditional school."

---

were proceeding at their own pace without the burden of an external evaluation.

So, you mothers of kindergarteners, I would like you to flip through this book and say to yourself, "That's nice. When my children are older and grading becomes an issue for me, I'm glad I'll have some tools I can use to understand the process and put it into practice." Then put this book on the shelf. Follow your child's pace. Enjoy it.

Upper Elementary Students? Maybe.

As children mature, they begin to take responsibility for their own learning. We rarely toss a few books at them and say, "OK, you're on your own." It becomes a partnership. Parents must teach and children must learn. By upper elementary, sometime between fourth and sixth grade, students exhibit enough maturity to be held accountable for parts of their education. Grading might help your children absorb content and develop study and time-management skills.

Junior High Students? Yes.

Grading should be practiced in junior high. Most children are old enough to enjoy the benefits formal grading will bring in terms of accountability and time management. When you begin formal evaluation, in upper elementary or junior high, begin slowly. Pick one subject, perhaps math, and develop a plan. Experiment. Once you are comfortable, add another subject. If you move slowly, you will have time to "ramp up," as they say in the business world.

High School Students? Definitely.

Depending on the student and his future plans, grading becomes very important in high school. If you have a high school student and are just beginning to grade, take the time to develop a plan, but also give yourself permission to change it if necessary. With time and adjustment, you will gain confidence in your ability to evaluate your children.

❧Your Personal Grading Philosophy

How does your family view grading? What do you hope the grade accomplishes? How will it benefit your school experience?

Parents who follow a relaxed form of schooling tend to be lenient and informal with their grades and rely primarily on subjective criteria. Students earn A's easily. Less-demanding grading scales are preferred. On the other hand, those who follow more structured forms tend to be more demanding and rely on more objective means. A's are very difficult to obtain, requiring a great deal of labor. Grading scales tend to promote mastery. Where a 70 percent for a family following a less-structured approach to education might earn a C, this same 70 percent might be recorded as an F by a family with a highly structured philosophy of education. Your educational philosophy will determine your grading philosophy.

❧How to Use this Book

This book is designed to help you understand grading and evaluation. Be forewarned—it covers a lot of ground. Therefore, everything in this book will not apply directly to you at this particular time in your homeschool journey. In fact, you will want to read it over several times in the years to come.

Part One

The first part of this book, Chapters One through Nine, contains foundational information. Resist the temptation to skip ahead to the subject areas. The especially important Chapter Four, "The Three Grading Components," examines the three ingredients needed to formulate grades: definitions of each grade (A, B, C, D, and F), how to set up course plans, and using both partial and impartial criteria.

Other portions of Part One consider why you should grade and what makes it hard. We will review testing along with other grading methods and when to use each. Finally, we will examine the place of attitude, effort, ethics, and record keeping. Part One ends with ideas to begin formal grading.

Part Two

Part Two applies the ideas presented in Part One. We will discuss evaluation methods that work well for each subject and others that fall short. Additionally, we will discuss unique challenges, such as how to evaluate performances or lab reports. Part Two adapts Part One's methods and applies them to specific situations.

❧Freedom!

Frequently you will encounter the word *freedom* on the pages of this book. No, it did not escape the editor; it is deliberate. If I could convey only one thought to you, it would be that *you* are in charge of your children's education. You have great teaching freedom.

However, this might not be absolute freedom. When determining future goals and plans, you might consider a direction, such as college preparation, that will limit your freedom. Additionally, you might belong to a private school umbrella program, correspondence school, or accountability group which has its own requirements. If your purpose and philosophy are in line with the authority you have put yourself under, these organizations will help you reach your objectives because they give you the freedom to do what you ought.

Even so, grading is complex. I pray that you will find help and direction in these pages. I pray that you will find the tools you need. I will say this again:

This book contains suggestions. Homeschooling gives you the ability to design a course that reflects your family's personal philosophy of education. Grading measures and states how well your child met the goals, plans, and objectives you set for the course. Some of the suggestions presented here will not mesh with your philosophy. Leave them. Others will work well. Use them. Some will spark other creative ideas of your own. Adapt them. Above all, remember the Lord's admonition to the Galatians:

Stand fast therefore in the liberty wherewith Christ hath made us free, and be not entangled again with the yoke of bondage (Gal. 5:1).

Chapter *2*
God Grades

Modern dictionaries define *grade* as "a number or letter indicating the relative quality of a student's work in a course, examination, or special assignment" or "a mark assigned to a pupil by a teacher to indicate the degree of excellence attained." Synonyms include mark, rating, measure, evaluation, score, average, and ratio.

This definition lacks a key idea: by what standard? What determines the work's "relative quality"? In our postmodern society, we need to emphasize the concept of a standard. Consequently, in our discussion we will expand the absolute meaning of the term *grade*.

❧Definition

Grade: A number or letter assigned to the total or a portion of a student's work (such as an exam, project, or assignment), which measures and evaluates the degree to which the student has become proficient in the goals and objectives set for the course. A grade is an evaluation.

❧Biblical Grading

For a more thorough definition, we will turn to the Bible and see what it says. Is the concept of grading Biblical? Does it line up with the principles in God's Word? Or does it contradict them? Properly understood and implemented, grading completely aligns with God's Word.

Although the Bible does not discuss "grading" or any of the other modern words associated with it, it does talk of

- ❋ **weighing:** TEKEL: You have been weighed in the balances, and found wanting (Daniel 5:27).

- ❋ **measuring:** from whom the whole body, joined and knit together by what every joint supplies, according to the effective working [measurement] by which every part does its share, causes growth of the body for the edifying of itself in love (Ephesians 4:16).

- ❋ **testing:** And you shall remember that the LORD your God led you all the way these forty years in the wilderness, to humble you and test you, to know what was in your heart, whether you would keep His commandments or not (Deuteronomy 8:2).

- ❋ **examining:** I, the LORD, search the heart, I test the mind, even to give every man according to his ways, according to the fruit

---

> *A Mentor Mom Shares*
> ## HOW WE MADE THE GRADE
> "I really appreciated that chart about the kings of Judah and the fact that in a way, there was a grading criteria—a standard that one either met, or sort of met, or didn't meet at all. It is interesting to think that God has all kinds of tests He puts us through; and not just pencil and paper tests, like math or spelling."

of his doings (Jeremiah 17:10).

We could summarize these verses under the heading of what the Bible refers to as "judgment," in the sense of evaluation rather than condemnation.

❧Learning From the Master

Further, although not specifically called grading, God gives us an example of this judgment in His evaluation of the kings of Judah. God sums up the administration of each king in one or two sentences which form a ranking of sorts (see chart).

The highest ranking is reserved for those kings who met God's highest standard and were comparable to King David, a man after God's own heart (Acts 13:22). God describes several of the kings of Judah, including Asa, Hezekiah, and Josiah, as walking in the way of King David.

Jehoshaphat, who did right in the sight of the Lord but did not remove the high places, appears in the middle. In the summary statement, God describes Jehoshaphat as walking in the way of his father, Asa. Although a good king, he fell short of King David.

Next come the four kings Joash, Amaziah, Uzziah, and Jotham. The series begins with Joash, who did right in the sight of the Lord only as long as the priest Johoiada instructed him. After Johoiada's death, King Joash fell into great sin. King Amaziah did not follow the Lord with a whole heart. He did right in the sight of the Lord but not like King David. Uzziah walked in the way of Amaziah, but he was afflicted with leprosy for disobedience and spent his last years in seclusion. His son, Jotham, walked in the way of Uzziah. None of these kings removed the high places.

Finally, the phrase that sums up the reign of eleven kings contains the words, "and he did evil in the sight of the Lord…" These kings fell significantly short of God's standard.

By examining this ranking, we come to a number of conclusions. First, there was a standard by which all of the kings were measured: King David. Second, although eight kings were described as "good," they were not all equally good. The first three kings were better than Jehoshaphat, who was higher than the remaining four. Finally, eleven kings did not meet God's minimum standard and consequently failed.

Putting this information in modern terms we could easily assign each one of these kings a "grade." The first four could earn A's, 4.0, or the term "superior," depending on the method of summary we choose. Jehoshaphat could earn a B, 3.0, or rating of "very good." The next four could get C's, 2.0's, or be rated "good." While no kings earned a D or 1.0, the final eleven could be awarded F's, 0's, or the term "fail." Additionally, on this scale we could define the minimum acceptable grade as C, 2.0, or "good."

God grades. His evaluation of the kings of Judah exemplifies the process.

ᕭTo Make the Grade

In reality, nearly everyone is graded, evaluated, or measured every day. It is part of life. Customers rate salespeople. Bosses judge employees. Parents measure children. From the dinners we cook to the way we drive our cars, we are continually subject to the scrutiny and evaluation of others as well as ourselves. However, grading is hard. We will tackle why in the next chapter.

A Mentor Mom Shares
HOW WE MADE THE GRADE

"Grading was hard for me, just learning how to do it. I had no idea where to start. The way I teach differs from a traditional classroom setting, where teachers use an abundance of tests. We do a lot of practical life things, a lot of living learning and not many tests."

God's Evaluation Criteria for the Kings of Judah

Scale:

A = Did right in the sight of the Lord, like David.
B = Did right in the sight of the Lord, but did not remove the high places.
C = Did right, but not with a whole heart. High places not removed.

D = Not used.
F = Did evil in the sight of the Lord.

King	Reference (NASV)	Grade
Rehoboam	"And he did evil because he did not set his heart to seek the Lord" (2 Chronicles 12:12).	F
Abijam	"He walked in all the sins of his father which he had committed before him; and his heart was not wholly devoted to the LORD his God, like the heart of his father David" (2 Kings 15:3).	F
Asa	"And Asa did what was right in the sight of the Lord, like David his father" (2 Kings 15:11).	A
Jehoshaphat	"And he walked in the way of his father Asa and did not depart from it, doing right in the sight of the Lord. The high places, however, were not removed; the people had not yet directed their hearts to the God of their fathers" (2 Chronicles 20:32-33).	B
Jehoram	"And he walked in the way of the kings of Israel, just as the house of Ahab had done, for the daughter of Ahab became his wife; and he did evil in the sight of the Lord" (2 Kings 8:18).	F
Ahaziah	"And he did evil in the sight of the Lord like the house of Ahab, for they were his counselors after the death of his father, to his destruction" (2 Chronicles 22:4).	F
Joash	"And Joash did what was right in the sight of the Lord all the days in which Johoiada the priest instructed him. Only the high places were not taken away; the people still sacrificed and burned incense on the high places" (2 Kings 12:2-3).	C
Amaziah	"And he did right in the sight of the Lord, yet not with a whole heart." 2 Chronicles 25:2 "And he did right in the sight of the Lord, yet not like David his father; he did according to all that Joash his father had done. Only the high places were not taken away; the people still sacrificed and burned incense on the high places" (2 Kings 14:3).	C
Uzziah	"And he did right in the sight of the Lord according to all that his father Amaziah had done. Only the high places were not taken away; the people still sacrificed and burned incense on the high places" (2 Kings 15:3-4).	C
Jotham	"And he did what was right in the sight of the Lord, he did according to all that his father Uzziah had done. Only the high places were not taken away; the people still sacrificed and burned incense on the high places" (2 Kings 15:34-35).	C
Ahaz	"… and he did not do right in the sight of the Lord as David his father had done" (2 Chronicles 28:1).	F

Hezekiah	"And he did right in the sight of the Lord, according to all that his father David had done" (2 Chronicles 29:2).	A
Manasseh	"And he did evil in the sight of the Lord according to the abominations of the nations whom the Lord dispossessed before the sons of Israel" (2 Chronicles 33:2).	F
Amon	"And he did evil in the sight of the Lord as Manasseh his father had done, and Amon sacrificed to all the carved images which his father Manasseh had made, and he served them" (I Chronicles 33:22).	F
Josiah	"And he did right in the sight of the Lord, and walked in the ways of his father David and did not turn aside to the right or to the left" (2 Chronicles 34:2).	A
Johoahaz	"And he did evil in the sight of the Lord, according to all that his fathers had done" (2 Kings 23:32).	F
Johoiakim	"… and he did evil in the sight of the Lord his God" (2 Chronicles 36:5).	F
Jehoiachin	"...and he did evil in the sight of the Lord according to all that his fathers had done" (2 Kings 23:37).	F
Zedekiah	"And he did evil in the sight of the Lord his God" (2 Chronicles 36:11).	F

A Mentor Mom Shares
HOW WE MADE THE GRADE

"My sister-in-law homeschooled for several years, then she had to put her kids in school because her health was so poor. She said, 'You know, my husband was never interested when I gave the grades. I'd say, "O.K., Honey" and hand him the grades. He never looked at them. Now that the kids attend school, he really wants to see those report cards.' That really bugged her. She thought, 'Why weren't you interested when I set the grades?' I think it goes back to parent familiarity. You know your children. You want to know what someone else thinks."

A Mentor Mom Shares
HOW WE MADE THE GRADE

"I found it helpful to take the mystery out of grading, to break it down into its component parts, and see how each step is done. Suddenly it's not so mysterious anymore. Then when I actually do it, I feel comfortable—it's not such a big deal. God gives me strength each day to keep going. I think of the scripture, 'Faithful is He who calls you and He will also bring it to pass' (II Thessalonians 5:24). OK, He's called me to do this. He's going to give me what it takes."

Chapter 3
Hard, But Worth It

Some parents resist grading their students at all. Their argument goes something like this, "Grades are a deterrent to learning. I just want my child to do his best, not work for some arbitrary mark. If I grade him, he won't develop a love of learning for its own sake." On the surface, this statement rings true. In some situations a child learns only what he needs to pass a test, then promptly forgets it. In this case, he does work for the grade rather than for the knowledge.

This argument loses its ring with a proper view of the child and the purpose of grading. Every child is a sinner. Unfortunately, so is every parent. Without an evaluation standard the parent becomes as arbitrary as the grade might seem to be. Rather than do his best, the student learns to get by. In fact, if minimal effort on his part already earns A's, why should he work any harder?

In my home town a straight, flat, deserted road beckons drivers to exceed the speed limit. Sometimes a patrolman works nearby, checking drivers' speed and issuing tickets. At other times he leaves a large electronic speed indicator. As a driver approaches, the sign prominently displays his current speed. Speeders slow down immediately. Like that speed sign, grades give students the information and feedback they need to improve. Yes, grading is hard, but is worthwhile.

✑Who is Being Graded?

The first difficulty with grading became very clear to me a little while ago. A group of us were on a field trip and a docent asked our homeschooled students some questions. The students did very well, supplying well-reasoned, insightful answers. Then the docent asked a particularly hard question, one that required a great deal of thought. Several attempted it and stumbled. Finally one young man provided a correct answer. Several of us murmured in approval.

His mother, however, raised her arm in a victory salute. At first I thought she was congratulating her son. Then it hit me: she was congratulating *herself*. Thinking back, I have seen the same reaction from many moms and have often felt it myself. We are proud of ourselves when our children make progress. And rightly so. But could this same feeling follow us as we evaluate our students' progress? Instead of grading them, are we really, at least partially, grading ourselves? Do we feel we have failed if our students earn less than an A? Are we giving ourselves that A?

In another example, my daughter and I taught a California history class together. She was in charge of the geography. After introducing 25 of California's geographical features, she administered a quiz. Most of the students did not do well. When we got home, my daughter wanted to know if that was her fault, a result of poor teaching. Not entirely. All of my classes do poorly on this first quiz, but it usually spurs them on to greater effort. Certainly, my daughter needed to provide clear, understandable teaching, but the students were obliged to take responsibility for their part of the learning. Both sides could improve.

When it comes to grading, could we be losing sight of the fact that although we must teach, children must learn? We must provide clear, forthright teaching in a manner the child can grasp. We must strive to help our children conquer those difficult concepts. But students must strive, as well. Grading concerns this second half, the students' responsibility. When we grade, we measure our students against the objectives we set for the course. We measure our own efforts elsewhere.

✑Who Sets the Standard?

The second grading problem homeschoolers encounter concerns the preconceived notions surrounding the term "grade." Most of our experience comes from the traditional school system. We think somewhere "out there" is the way to determine grades, and we feel we must abandon our freedom to educate our children in the way God has called and come under the authority of this nebulous standard.

No universal standard exists. If we have high school students who plan to attend a four-year college or university directly upon graduation, we might elect to pursue "college prep" courses. Since colleges have certain expectations and assumptions for these courses, we need to be aware of their requirements. For all other classes, we have much more freedom in grading because we design our own courses and grading criteria.

This is the key. Our grading criteria should be derived from our course plans and objectives. Realizing that we have a great deal of liberty, constrained only by the laws of our state and the Biblical necessity that all must be Christ-centered, we need to realize that we also have complete freedom to set the standard by which we appraise our children's progress.

✑Comparatively Speaking

Another difficulty with grading concerns comparison.

Because of the influence of traditional schooling, we think grading should compare our children with others. To determine whether an assignment is worth an A, B, or C, we feel we need several "typical" examples so we can determine our students' placement. Instead, when we grade, we should be comparing our children with a standard in line with God's principles. The Bible speaks of this in 2 Corinthians 10:12-13:

> *For we dare not class ourselves or compare ourselves with those who commend themselves. But they, measuring themselves by themselves, and comparing themselves among themselves, are not wise. We, however, will not boast beyond measure, but within the limits of the sphere which God appointed us—a sphere which especially includes you.*

This verse specifically commands us *not* to compare our children with others. Rather, we are to measure according to the standard.

❧And Now for the Benefits

By all means, grading *is* hard, especially for home-schoolers. Unlike classroom teachers who develop a

---

A Mentor Mom Shares

HOW WE MADE THE GRADE

"Grading has been a lot better than I anticipated. It gives me the opportunity to stop, sit down, examine where am I headed, and why, and determine what I want my children to get out of the course. It also shows me their strengths and weaknesses.

"This was very clear when I did language arts grades last semester for my son. I was on autopilot, doing the same old thing. When I had to stop and actually grade him, I realized that he's falling far short of where I want him to be—not so much because he can't do the work or is choosing not to; it's mainly because I'm not holding the standard up high enough and showing him, 'This is what I expect. This is where I want you to be.' For me it was a real wakeup call. It has helped me to focus on those areas and think, 'I need to pay attention to this for the rest of this year and for planning next year.' I'm trying to push him without frustrating him."

---

standard which they might use over and over again, we usually need one for each course and for each student. In future chapters we will discuss ways to make this easier, but we need to ask ourselves, "Why should we grade? Are there any benefits to grading?" Indeed, there are.

Transfer of Responsibility

Grades transfer responsibility for learning from the parent to the child. Years ago, I taught my older son to clean the house. He would do a slightly haphazard job, then ask me to come check. I would point out what he had missed and he would expend more effort. If I missed telling him something the first time, he would strenuously object if I pointed it out on the second. After several weeks of this I realized he was not learning to clean; rather, he was learning to do the minimum amount that would be acceptable to me at the time. So, I tried something different. I carefully explained what a clean room looked like. I set a standard. Then, it was up to him to strive to meet the standard. He could evaluate his own progress and determine what else, if anything, he needed to do.

Interestingly, interpersonal conflict decreased as a result of this experiment. No longer did he have to please me, or live up to my sometimes arbitrary conception of a "clean room." Some days that idea might have been higher than others, such as when we were expecting company. Instead, he had an objective, unchanging standard by which he could determine whether or not he was finished. I am not saying we never had other problems in this area ☺, but they significantly decreased.

In the same way, if students take responsibility for their learning, they need to know our expectations. Standards help them to know what they need to accomplish, while keeping teachers consistent.

Benefits to Parents

Parents might also use grades to improve their teaching abilities. While doing chores with my older son, I realized that further instruction was necessary in certain areas. Likewise, if a student scores poorly on a particular assignment, a parent would know she needs to re-teach the material, perhaps approaching it in a different manner (throwing out the low score, as well).

Academic Translation

Grades meet the objective of translating the homeschool experience into a format familiar to other educators. At some point, most parents will have to give an account of their students' experience in order to further their education. When communicating with others in the academic world, we need to be sure we use the same language. Report cards, transcripts, and course descriptions take our unique homeschooling experience and record it in a format familiar to others. We need to maintain integrity with our account, but we also need to communicate accurately.

Additionally, grades (plus credits for high schoolers) can be a safeguard. Although our plan might be to homeschool through high school, the vagaries of life are many. It is possible to enter some public and private schools without grades, but schools might require an entrance test to assess placement. Others might not accept certain classes and require them to be redone. Grades and credits are no guarantee, but they do make your child's educational experience appear to be more valid. Remember, *A man's heart plans his way, But the LORD directs his steps (Proverbs 16:9)*.

A Mentor Mom Shares
HOW WE MADE THE GRADE

"**B**ecause I'm a product of the public school system, I believed only a credentialed teacher could assign a letter grade to a child's work. I've had to work through feeling guilty if I give my children all good grades. 'Well, of course you're going to give good grades,' you can hear a stranger saying, 'You're their parent.' They don't believe I'm objective or even qualified. But it's pretty straightforward, especially if I've figured out ahead of time how I'm going to grade. The mystery vanishes when I realize how simple grading is.

"When my husband and I were newly married, he was teaching at Cal Poly and grading a course at finals time. He asked me, 'What do you think of this student? This one is really borderline. He was never at any of the classes. He only came twice, he took the midterm and got an 89, and really didn't put forth the effort. I could give him a B or bump him up to an A. What should I do?' I realized then there was some subjectiveness to this teachers grading thing. We talked about it and he gave him a B. Later on there was another student who was the opposite. This kid worked so hard and got an 89, but he'd been to everything. So he bumped him up to the A. That shocked me, because here I had gone through Cal Poly thinking grades were entirely objective."

Especially For High School
Finally, special considerations for high school students include the following:
1. Grades and credits satisfy the admission requirements of colleges which are based on a combination of GPA (grade point average), and SAT (Scholastic Aptitude Test) scores. If a GPA is not available, colleges will give more weight to SAT (or ACT Assessment) scores, which could work to some students' disadvantage.
2. Grades are required for many scholarship, grant and loan programs.
3. With a GPA of 3.0 or above, many students are eligible for a good driver discount on their insurance rates.

ᔐTo Make the Grade

A couple of years ago I attended a journalism convention in New Mexico. While talking with teachers from schools across the nation, I was frequently asked how many "preps" I had. I was not sure since I did not know what a prep was. It turns out it is the number of classes a teacher has to prepare for. If I am teaching the same science course to four different classes, it counts as one prep. The task will be easier if I have taught this course before, because I will only have to update and refine previously prepared lesson plans. The teachers

A Mentor Mom Shares
HOW WE MADE THE GRADE

"I think grading has helped my high school daughter a little bit with time management. She realizes she needs to adjust her schedule to spend more time on things that are weighted more heavily. If she can't work on something this week, she has to budget her time, planning to work on the weekend or pushing it into the following week. She can think, 'OK, this is due in this subject, and that is due in that. This assignment is a big deal and I absolutely have to get it in on time. Because it's worth so much, I want to spend more time on it to make sure I do my best.' I'm not saying she then looks at another assignment and says, 'OK, I can slide on this,' but she doesn't need to allow it as much time. She gives the first assignment a higher priority."

who thought they had a full load had three or four preps.

That year I had sixteen. My son, who has since graduated, took nine classes (some only a semester in length) over the course of the year, while my daughter had seven. I prepared for each and every one because I had never taught the subjects before. This year, with only one student, I still have eight. Even though I am teaching the same subjects, my approach is as different as my student.

In thinking of grading, sometimes we feel constrained by the procedures used in schools. As homeschoolers, we cannot copy schools' methods. We would be overwhelmed. Instead, we need to look for value in the model, then formulate our own criteria to correspond to the objectives we have set for the course.

For the present, we need to recognize that although grading is work, it includes benefits. Grading brings us to a new frontier, one which we enter relying on the Lord. He will stretch us as He continues to equip us to minister to the children He has entrusted to our care.

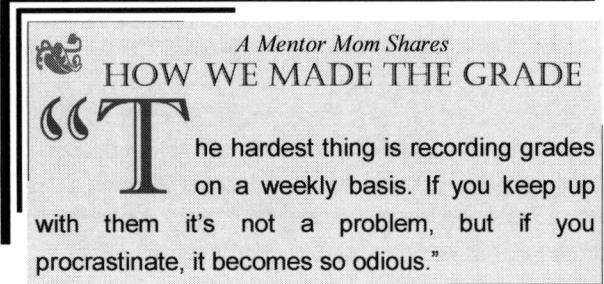

A Mentor Mom Shares
HOW WE MADE THE GRADE

"The hardest thing is recording grades on a weekly basis. If you keep up with them it's not a problem, but if you procrastinate, it becomes so odious."

Chapter 4
The Three Components

So far, we have discussed grading in generalities, including the definition of the term *grade*, the Biblical perspective, some misconceptions in our thinking which might make grading harder than it should be, and the benefits we are likely to experience when we evaluate. Now we are ready to discuss the three components necessary to determine grades.

First, since a grade is simply an alphabetic or numeric summary which evaluates a student's work, we should make sure we understand the definition of an A, B, C, D, and F. Second, since the grade measures the student's progress towards the outcomes set for the course, we will discuss how well-defined plans are crucial to determining grades. Finally, since the grade measures the degree to which the student becomes proficient, we will begin our discussion on grading methods by defining the difference between *objective* and *subjective* grading criteria.

❧What's in a Name?

Grades communicate information. But, in a way, they are words from a foreign language or new vocabulary terms. When we assign marks, what do they mean? What information do they convey? In words, here are the definitions for each particular grade category (these are also listed in Appendix A):

A - **Superior**. Work reflects a level of accomplishment significantly above the minimum. Excellent, first rate, of the highest order, very remarkable, extraordinary, marvelous, wonderful, splendid, standout, outstanding, striking, supreme, the best, first-class, prime, admirable, noteworthy

B - **Above average**. The student has done more than just complete the assignments or course work. Very good, fine, quality, choice, solid, precise, accurate, detailed, careful, meticulous, particular, worthy, meritorious, estimable, praiseworthy, competent, commendable

C - **Average**. Work meets, but does not exceed, the requirements. Good, satisfactory, acceptable, serviceable, presentable, admissible, medium, good enough, passable, up to par, tolerable, permissible, allowable, all right, suitable, fair, OK, middling, minimum, lowest acceptable, adequate

D - **Below average**. Work is inadequate. Insufficient, too little, not enough, wanting, mediocre, inferior, below par, unsatisfactory, disappointing, unsuitable, flawed, faulty, deficient, lacking, meager, scanty, marginal

F - **Fail**. Work fell significantly short of the requirements. Poor, failing, not acceptable, not passing.

In my experience, homeschoolers approach these definitions in one of two ways. First, through lack of instruction, they do not understand and properly use the established definitions of the letter grades. Many times, work that meets the minimum course standard receives an A. However, by definition, C level work meets course requirements. An A denotes "superior," "outstanding," "first-class," or "the best." Additionally, parents might consider C a failing grade, but by definition F reflects "failing" or "not passing." According to the definition accepted in educational circles, C means "good," "satisfactory," "average," or "up to par." Finally, a good number of homeschool parents only utilize two grades: A and F (or sometimes A and C). Work earns an A if the student met the requirements of the course, and an F if he did not. By definition, these kinds of courses would be designated "pass/fail." Work which met the course requirements would be awarded a passing grade (P) while that which did not would fail (F).

Second, homeschoolers redefine grades. Instead of using the set definitions, they come up with their own. For one parent, an A might designate excellent or superior work, while for another it represents acceptable or satisfactory performance. "My definitions differ from yours," these parents argue. "I have the right to set my own labels and don't have to adhere to any pre-established definitions."

Although parents might not realize it, this is a deconstructionist argument, a way of thinking in which standards do not apply. For the deconstructionist, words have no meaning and are open to interpretation and redefinition. Therefore, one person's definition of the word "is" can differ from another's.

This "is" dangerous! When we redefine words using our own reason, truth becomes relative. No longer is Jesus Christ the Word and the Bible the inerrant, inspired word of God. The term "sin" can be redefined depending on each person's whim, so that the term "salvation" becomes meaningless. Although redefining the vocabulary of grading might not have the same impact as redefining Biblical words, the same principles apply. Christians, called to a high, ethical standard, do not have the option of changing the language.

✎Three Characteristics of Good Objectives

Once we understand the vocabulary of evaluation, we need to decide what to teach. This includes our objectives for each course—what we hope to accomplish, and how that accomplishment will be measured. Here, in contrast to grade definitions, we have a great deal of liberty. Rather than spend time on areas the students have mastered, parents can concentrate on those requiring more effort. Each course may be specifically tailored to the students' and parent's immediate and long-term goals.

A Mentor Mom Shares
HOW WE MADE THE GRADE

"I make sure my goals are really clear. That helps me the most, because I can see if we've missed them. If I know what my goals are and know what an A stands for, then I can look at my children's work and see what they've earned. Some of it is trial and error, because I have to get involved to determine what I really want. I would say, know your materials and your child. Give thought to your goals as a family. Look at examples of other people's goals and their grading systems.

"When I saw Barbara Shelton's [*Senior High: A Home-Designed Form+U+la*] criteria, I saved it because it made so much sense to me. Her criteria were written out so I could see what needed to be done to achieve each grade. She had some definite goals. For a C she said, 'Complete all course work' and she added extras to bring the grade up to a B or an A—things that were important to her. If you get ideas from the different ways people grade, it helps. However, I worried for years, 'What are all the other people doing?' Now I realize it doesn't matter what others are doing. It only matters what my child does weighed against his abilities and what he was doing at the beginning of the year."

The more time you spend formulating course descriptions with clear outcomes, the easier your grading task. In the next chapter we will discuss how to develop good course objectives. First, we need to know what a good objective or goal looks like. Whenever possible, our plans need to have three characteristics; they must be

reachable,
measurable,
and specific.

I press toward the goal for the prize of the upward call of God in Christ Jesus (Phil. 3:14).

Reachable

First of all, can our purpose be reached? Prodigies aside, first graders cannot learn algebra. Students are not ready for algebra before they master basic math, and until that time, algebra must wait. Elementary, you might say, but sometimes we ask more from our children than they are able to give. For example, we might ask our children to write a five paragraph essay. If the student has had little or no writing instruction, the task is impossible. Instead, we would need to break it down into smaller segments:

* Write three body paragraphs. All must have topic or transition sentences and good organization.
* Experiment with several ways to write an introductory paragraph.
* Learn to write a satisfying conclusion which brings the essay to a close.

Objectives might be unattainable for other reasons. To illustrate, say that plans for a history class included the following:

* Develop a love and appreciation for the rich heritage of our nation.

This worthy, admirable objective might be reachable, but it has another problem. It falls outside the teacher's control. Teachers may not dictate their students' thoughts. You cannot require a student to love and appreciate our nation's history. You can show him why you do and why he should, but the change has to come from him.

Further, how would you determine a grade for this idealistic aim? How would you know when he appreciates his nation's heritage? How would you determine the difference between superior, very good, or good appreciation? What an impossible task!

Although parents would be delighted to see this response to a history class, for evaluation purposes it doesn't work. It might be helpful to differentiate between *ideal aims* and *attainable aims*:

* Ideal aims are those sometimes unreachable, somewhat idealistic, "pie in

the sky," aims or intents for a course. Although worthy and commendable, they are fuzzy. It is difficult to say when or whether an ideal aim has been achieved.

* Attainable aims are precise statements of the objectives for the course which are reachable via the teaching cycle. An ideal aim for a Bible course might be for the child to receive Jesus Christ as his Lord and Savior. Although a great objective, as an attainable aim it has problems. A teacher can lead and enlighten, but only the Holy Spirit can change his heart, and only the child can receive His precious gift. Conversely, an attainable aim for the Bible course might be to follow Paul's steps on his second missionary journey, locate the cities he visited on a map, or memorize his sermon on Mars Hill (Acts 17:22-34).

Many times we will (and should) have ideal aims for our children. These comprise the areas of character, career, physical, mental, and academics. We hope our children will attain all of our ideal aims. However, for grading and evaluation purposes, ideal aims are less than ideal.

Measurable

When traveling with our younger children, my husband and I frequently heard, "Are we there yet?" We need to ask ourselves the same question with our objectives. How will we know when we have arrived? There must be some way of determining whether or not our objectives have been met. Sometimes parents will formulate objectives like this:

* Draw close to the Lord Jesus as student studies the hand of the Lord in history.

While completely admirable, this outcome cannot be measured. How will we know when our children have drawn close to the Lord Jesus? Will there ever be a time we can say that 100 percent of this goal has been reached? Instead, this process occurs over a lifetime.

Objectives might be measured by quality, quantity, or both. Quality concerns how well the aim was met, while quantity deals with the number of required tasks. Objectives concerning how well a task was completed (quality) include the following:

* Complete a page of multiplication calculations with two or fewer errors.

* Score at least 80 percent on a chapter review test.

* Two weeks after a spelling lesson, be able to correctly spell words in dictated sentences with a 90 percent accuracy.

* Write a book report which explores how the author used description, dialogue, and action to bring the story's characters to life.

Although the last item in the above list might not seem to be measurable and rather open to interpretation, it can be measured by subjective means. In a subsequent section of this chapter, we will explore the difference between impartial and partial ways of evaluation.

Quantifiable objectives are also measurable, except that they deal with amounts rather than value, or quantity rather than quality. Plans which concern how many tasks must be completed (quantity) include the following:

* Perform aerobic exercise at least 30 minutes each day, four days a week.

* Collect at least five rocks in each of the following categories: igneous, metamorphic, sedimentary.

* Write five essays.

* Analyze three novels in depth.

Again, although the last item on this list might require some subjective means to determine what constitutes "in depth" analysis, I will save this discussion until later.

Specific

Finally, good plans must be definite. Often homeschoolers, especially inexperienced homeschoolers, will formulate objectives like these:

* Complete two textbooks or
* Finish fifth grade arithmetic

Although *perhaps* reachable and measurable, these plans lack precision. What does "complete" mean? Must the student simply read the textbook, or must he also demonstrate understanding? Has the student "finished fifth grade arithmetic" when June arrives? How will the parent know the goals have been met?

In *Alice's Adventures in Wonderland* by Lewis Carroll, Alice loses her way and asks the Cheshire Cat for directions.

"Would you tell me, please, which way I ought to walk from here?"

"That depends a good deal on where you want to get to," said the Cat.

"I don't much care where," said Alice.

"Then it doesn't matter which way you walk," said the Cat.

"—so long as I get *somewhere*," Alice added as an explanation.

"Oh, you're sure to do that," said the Cat, "if you only walk long enough."

With perseverance, we complete the textbook and reach the end of the year. Like Alice, we end up somewhere. Good objectives, however, provide a road map. They contain detail:

* Understand and list the differences between the American War for Independence and the French Revolution.
* Learn the major phylum and characteristics of the kingdom *plantae*.
* Write concise paragraph summaries of short stories read.

When creating course plans for grading purposes, you should make sure your plans are reachable, measurable, and specific. If you spend adequate time on this step, you will find it easier to grade and evaluate your child.

ᨠObjective vs. Subjective Criteria

Grading criteria complete the list of the three necessary ingredients for grading and evaluation. Once we understand the vocabulary and know how to recognize well-stated objectives, we decide how to award the grades and what constitutes an A, B, or C. While we will continue discussing this subject in future chapters, for the present we will limit ourselves to one area only: the difference between *objective* and *subjective* criteria.

Objective criteria judge work according to an easily identifiable standard. For example

* right or wrong comprehension question answers
* correctly or incorrectly spelled or defined vocabulary words
* correct or incorrect dates, places, and names
* right or wrong geographical locations

Objective criteria help in subjects such as math and English. Additionally, they contribute when discussing the content (as opposed to application or evaluation) of subjects such as history and science or when dealing with lower-level critical thinking skills (see the discussion on Bloom's Taxonomy in Chapter Five).

Subjective criteria, on the other hand, evaluate and judge work using feelings or impressions. Standards can vary by individuals and take into account personal taste, interests, and biases such as

* beauty, style, personal likes and dislikes
* completeness, effort expended, and attitude
* attendance and class contribution

Subjective criteria benefit evaluation of projects such as art, sewing, or auto mechanics, as well as devotions, performances (speech, piano), creative writing, and P.E.

I made up (I think) the term *quantified subjective* to describe the effort to turn subjective into objective criteria. Instead of evaluating the task in total, break it into smaller pieces and measure each using partial or impartial criteria. Not only will these smaller portions be easier to assess, you will also know when your children

need extra instruction. Examples of smaller components include the following:

* **Art:** Use of art principles (light, line, color, form, perspective, composition, balance).
* **Projects:** Measure of skill level; for example, sewing techniques. Perhaps some art components as above.
* **Performance:** Use of voice projection, expression, poise, articulation, confidence, content, and style.
* **PE:** Achievement of certain skills, persistence, and improvement.

As a result of our own schooling and the modernist philosophy then prevalent, we have a bias toward objective criteria. We view objective criteria as better or more scholarly than subjective criteria. "Real" teachers rely on objective criteria, we secretly think. Unless we do so as well, we cheat.

Not so. Subjective criteria have their place. In fact, some subjects can be evaluated in no other way. Additionally, by observing our students' activity, using intuition, sometimes we are able to arrive at an accurate, although subjective grade.

Several years ago while teaching writing, I formed a series of objectives for my class. As I taught the homeschooled students new concepts, I gave them ample opportunity to practice, then evaluated them based on criteria I developed. At least, that is how it was supposed to work.

Towards the end of the course, I fell way behind and was faced with a stack of writing to evaluate. To make matters worse, at least one student submitted

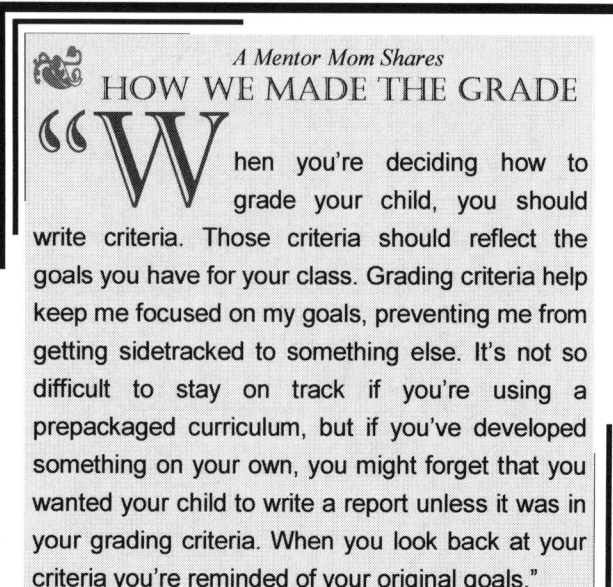

A Mentor Mom Shares
HOW WE MADE THE GRADE

"When you're deciding how to grade your child, you should write criteria. Those criteria should reflect the goals you have for your class. Grading criteria help keep me focused on my goals, preventing me from getting sidetracked to something else. It's not so difficult to stay on track if you're using a prepackaged curriculum, but if you've developed something on your own, you might forget that you wanted your child to write a report unless it was in your grading criteria. When you look back at your criteria you're reminded of your original goals."

several late papers. I made my way through the pile until only the "late" student was left. Contemplating my task I thought, "Based on the quality of his work [not his lateness], this student deserves a B." However, I could not quite bring myself to assign a grade without combing through each and every paper. Two hours later I had my grade. It was a B.

I am not suggesting that parents should use intuition to develop all grades. In this example, I had already given thought to the method I would use. I thought about what I wanted the students to achieve and wrote out the objectives for the course. Consequently, I had a feel for the quality of the student's work and my subjective evaluation was on the mark. You should exercise your educational freedom and use any combination of objective, subjective, or quantified subjective methods to award your students grades.

To Make the Grade

To grade, parents need to understand and use these three components:

- grade category definitions
- reachable, measurable, and specific objectives for each course
- a combination of objective and subjective evaluation criteria

Of the three, forming well-stated course plans gives the greatest difficulty. We will tackle this challenge in the next chapter.

Do You Hate Setting Goals?

Although I have studiously refrained from using the word *goal*, some of you might suspect that the word *objective* is a euphemism for goals. Does this term make you uneasy? Do you struggle to define course goals? In fact, do you really hate setting goals? If so, you are not alone.

According to Bobb Beihl, the author of *Stop Setting Goals*, up to 75 percent of us get pretty uncomfortable when asked to set goals. We would rather run three miles than complete the sentence, "At the end of this course, my child will be able to ..." However, we are great at identifying and solving problems.

Actually, you can create course objectives by setting goals or by solving problems. In the first, you look at the end result, while in the second you ask yourself, "What problems does my child need to overcome to learn this subject?" Let's walk through an example to see how this might happen. Say you want to develop an American history course.

The Goal-Setter

As a goal-setter, and after some research, you would envision your child's accomplishments by the end of the course. You want him to

- construct a century book with correct placement of historical figures and events;
- match people with their historical contribution, era, and world view;
- recognize and place geographical features; and
- complete a research report on some aspect of history such as a person, place, or event.

You then devise reachable, measurable, and specific objectives to reach these goals.

For example, you might specify what you want the century book to look like (simple or detailed entries, or drawings of each person or event, as well as how many you want to see included). For the research report you might think about length, number of references, number of quotes, or whatever else you would like to see.

The Problem-Solver

As a problem-solver, you would think to yourself, "My child knows nothing about American history and she should."

- You think, "She should have some understanding of the sequence of events and be able to place them in the correct half century. I know, I'll have her start a century book."

- Then you might think, "There are so many people to remember. I need to make a list of the ones I think are most important and decide what she should know about them, perhaps their historical contribution, era, and world view."

- Next, "I want her to become familiar with the geography of the eastern seaboard. She should be able to recognize and place geographical features such as major rivers, cities, and mountain ranges."

- Finally, you think, "You know, my child didn't do very well on the research report we tried last year. She could use a bit more practice and this might be a good place. I think I'll have her complete a research report on some aspect of history such as a person, place, or event."

Once you have these solutions to your problem, spend some time making them as reachable, measurable, and specific as you can to form objectives.

Objectives

Although the thinking differed, both approaches led to a similar outcome. Goal-setters see the forest and build trees. They see the overall plan at the beginning and determine steps to get there. Problem-solvers see trees and build a forest. They see individual steps and from these, form a plan. If you hate setting goals—stop! Solve problems, instead.

Chapter 5
Setting Course Objectives

If you have read Chapter Four, you know what a good objective looks like: reachable, measurable, and specific. Although fine in theory, what about in practice? How do you form and verbalize objectives for each of your children? I'm glad you asked! This chapter discusses how to create good course expectations. Discussion of evaluation techniques will begin in Chapter Six.

Where to Find Direction

As parents, we have numerous objectives for our children, including spiritual, character, social, thinking, and instructional. Although parents would do well to give thought to these areas, this discussion will stick with educational objectives. Where do you find them?

Basically, course expectations will fall into one of two categories: review/practice and new ground. There will be certain tasks you want your child to master. In math, your student will need to master decimals, fractions, and percents before he moves onto algebra. In English, he will need to master writing paragraphs

Goals vs. Problems

If the concept of problem-solving is new to you, it might be helpful to look at another example. Let's say you have a child approaching eleventh grade and you want to develop an American literature course for him.

1. As a goal-setter, you would envision your child's accomplishments by the end of the course. You want him to be familiar with a broad survey of American literature; recognize authors and match them to their works, era, and world view; be able to break the expanse of American literature into schools such as Puritan writers, transcendentalists, and Hudson River writers; and write competent essays that analyze the style and technique of each author. You then devise steps to reach these goals, what I'm calling objectives.

2. As a problem-solver, you would think to yourself, "My child knows nothing about American literature and she should. She should be familiar with the broad range of literature and authors from Puritan times to the present." Additionally, you might notice the wide perspective in American literature which would present another problem to solve: You would need to teach the various world views of the schools and guide your student in discernment. Finally, your child might have a problem writing analytical essays, especially with organization and using evidence to support her points. So, your third problem to solve would be to help her write analytical essays. The solutions to your problems become your objectives.

As you can see, although thinking differed, both approaches lead to a similar outcome.

About the Term "Objective"

Since so many people have an aversion to the term "goal," I tried not to use it very often. But what to use in its place? I got out my *Synonym Finder* and found

- aim
- purpose
- intent
- end
- objective
- target
- priority
- standard
- plan
- outcome
- expectation
- destination.

I selected "objective" because it seemed to have the least emotional connotation. However, if you object to objectives, select your preference from the above list. Then when you read about objectives, substitute whatever term will help you describe what you want to see your children accomplish in the course.

before he can begin reports. You know your child's abilities. Where does he need more practice? Keep track and make sure these areas are incorporated into your teaching plan.

In the other category, new ground, your objectives concern the next step, new concepts your students must learn. For example, building on a science foundation laid in elementary school, most junior high students take a life science course or an introduction to biology. The student studying music moves from learning the notes, to forming them on his instrument, to playing songs. When determining objectives, whether continuing or new instruction, you have a number of options.

1. Remember Your First Love

So often we run to the "experts" to see what we are "supposed" to teach. Avoid this temptation. First, run to our Lord. Spend time in prayer asking Him for direction. Search the scriptures for wisdom to discover His plan for the children He has given you. Formulate some ideal plans, then consider how these might be changed to

---

A Mentor Mom Shares
HOW WE MADE THE GRADE

"The criteria of a teacher who expects a lot from her student in the area of math, are going to be very different from someone whose child has learning difficulties. Would it be right for the parent of the child with learning difficulties to establish criteria reflecting the other parent's goals for her gifted child? It would be impossible for that child to ever earn an A or succeed. But the parent of a gifted child is right to expect more. We should all challenge and push our children according to their strengths and weaknesses, so they will become the best people they can be to the glory of God. You must establish your goals and grading criteria based on your children and the way the Lord leads you. Pray and ask Him, before you even choose your curriculum for the year, how you should establish your goals. Then, don't allow yourself to become sidetracked when you are tempted to compare your child's progress with another's. Look back at those God-ordained goals and objectives and work hard at being faithful to accomplish what you know God has called you to do."

---

attainable objectives. Above all, remember your purpose and why you were called to homeschool in the first place.

Oftentimes, the parent most responsible for the day-to-day teaching will set objectives by herself, without any input from her spouse. This is a mistake. Although God gives grace to single parents, He gave children two parents because that is what it takes. Whenever possible, both parents should seek the Lord's will for their children and devise objectives for the school year. An evening or weekend seeking the Lord's direction is likely to give a clear picture. If you ask for wisdom, He promises to give it.

2. Consider the Possibilities

Because of our own educational backgrounds, we do not always know how to teach specific subjects. When do students begin to write reports? What should an introduction include? What are transitions and when are they used? To educate ourselves, we might want to examine

- Scope and Sequence—a list of goals and objectives students should meet. All major publishers have scope and sequences which correlate with their textbooks. Be aware: no "correct" skill sequence exists, so these will greatly vary. Additionally, read scope and sequences with care. Many times tasks introduced in one grade recur in later years, permitting ample time for mastery.

- State Frameworks and Standards—a detailed list of objectives for each subject by grade level, developed for the public schools in each state. When used with care, they might provide benefits. Most state frameworks are available on the Internet. To find them, go to your favorite search engine and type the key words, "California" [or another state], "history" [or other subject], and "framework" [or "standards"].

- Cathy Duffy provides an excellent introduction to this subject in Chapter Two of her book, *Christian Home Educator's Curriculum Manual for Elementary Grades,* including a traditional scope and sequence for math and reading through grade eight, and suggestions for scope and sequence resources.

- The second half of Robin Scarlata's book, *What Your Child Needs to Know When,* contains several pages of detailed evaluation lists to help plan your course of study through grade eight.

With so many resources, parents should be encouraged by the flexibility they offer. These resources could be useful tools to derive personal, individual objectives.

3. Incorporate Critical Thinking Skills

All of us want our children to discern the difference between good and evil. We hope they will learn to think for themselves and evaluate all of life according to the revealed Word of God. But how do we teach this? Perhaps a short discussion of critical thinking skills might help.

Bloom's Taxonomy, developed by Benjamin Bloom, breaks thinking skills into six different categories as illustrated in the first chart at the end of this chapter. ("Taxonomy" means categorization.) Benjamin Bloom believed learning occurred in stages and "evolved" as children matured. He also put great stock in man's reason and ability. According to Bloom, the highest critical thinking skill was evaluating or judging, with man himself determining right and wrong. Christians know it is not man's place to determine right and wrong. Instead, we are called to apply God's Word to all of life.

Obviously Christians cannot endorse Bloom's presuppositions and find his taxonomy problematic. Nevertheless, Bloom's Taxonomy helps parents to understand different kinds of thinking. With maturity and instruction, children will be able to move from

* Lower levels of comprehension (Who was the first president of the United States?), to

* Thought (Why were losses so great during the War Between the States?), to

* Evaluation (According to the Bible, was the Gulf War a just war?)

These categories also help when we teach a new subject to children of any age. For example, to learn a foreign language, students must master the alphabet, rules, and basic vocabulary (knowledge and comprehension). Next, they begin to put these pieces together to converse (apply information) and translate (analyze information). Finally, they become proficient in the language and use it to write (synthesis) or study foreign books (evaluation).

By understanding the various learning steps as well as the deficiency in Bloom's presuppositions, you can profitably use Bloom's Taxonomy to help you set objectives.

4. Long-Range Plans

What does your child want to be when he grows up? Does he show any particular interests, talents or aptitudes? My husband is fond of saying (although not original to him), "The future determines the present." Simply put, this means that our future aspirations determine our present actions. For example, if we will teach seventh grade in the upcoming year, we need to research and purchase instructional materials. Our future plan (teaching seventh grade) determines our present action (obtaining resources). Similarly, if the child plans to attend college, his junior high and high school courses need to prepare him for that eventuality. A child with an aptitude for music might pursue a different course from the child with a talent in science and require different emphasis. Current objectives need to align with the child's long range plans.

5. Consider the Child

Homeschool parents know that all children learn at different rates. Your child might learn to read on his own while mine needs comprehensive phonics instruction. My child might master the art of writing with little effort, while yours needs hours of step-by-step instruction and practice. When forming our objectives, we need to consider the areas we would like to improve, as in the following:

* A student struggling with word problems in math might benefit from extra practice using a word problem booklet or workbook.

* A student making numerous mechanical errors on his English assignments might need a comprehensive grammar course.

Course objectives should provide for remediation of the student's weaknesses or teach him compensatory skills.

A Mentor Mom Shares
HOW WE MADE THE GRADE

"People need to make sure that their criteria are derived for their families and do not reflect what someone else expects from her child. When I first started to counsel with families, I could get discouraged because I would see what they were requiring of their family and think, 'Wow, that's way more than what we've done!' It made me feel that we're not doing enough and maybe that I should add this and that. Sometimes that's true, but I think we have to be careful not to compare ourselves too much, and really set aside that time in the spring or the early summer to pray and ask God what He wants. In a way, grades are meant to compare students with each other. But for us, they're a measurement of what our children have actually accomplished."

6. Narrow the Possibilities

A parent who has followed steps one through five above should be overwhelmed with possible objectives. Take comfort—they do not have to be completed in one year! Which skills are most important? Must the child master an area, or is exposure more suitable? Can certain plans be combined across subject areas? For example, can essays be practiced while answering literature or history questions? What must be accomplished this year and what might be postponed for the future?

Examine each objective and give it a priority. Those most important should receive a "1," including areas that must be mastered before further study is possible. Formulate a plan for these objectives. Those next in importance would receive a "2." These need to be incorporated into the teaching plan at some point, but not necessarily the following year. The final category, those designated with a "3," would have the lowest priority. They might include plans which would be good to complete if there was time.

By giving each objective a priority, parents narrow the possibilities and determine which to address. An example appears below.

Objective	Priority
Conduct an overview of American history	1
Learn basic science vocabulary	1
Teach anatomy (prerequisite: biology)	3
Teach biology	2
Take third year of foreign language	3
Master the cello	3
Become proficient in tennis	2

✎Practical Objective-Setting

After you have found direction and set objectives, you need to turn your statements of purpose into precise sentences. First, begin with a general statement articulating the intent of your course and why you are teaching it. Do not worry if it sounds ideal. For example, "Survey world history from the beginning to the Reformation, paying particular attention to God's judgment and grace, and the unveiling of the plan of salvation. Make the study interesting and memorable."

Next, ask yourself, "How am I going to get there?" Research available materials and make your choices. For this example, we will choose a textbook, *Streams of Civilization Volume I* (Christian Liberty Press). We will also choose four works of accurate, historical fiction by G.A. Henty.

Third, ask, "How am I going to use these resources? How am I going to know when I'm finished?" Develop outcomes for each resource. Perhaps your student needs to practice essays. For the textbook, at the end of each chapter, you might ask the student to respond in an open-book essay to one or more teacher-supplied questions. For the Henty books, you might require the student to write an essay comparing the events in the book to the historical record, noting which parts are fictional, accurate, or based on truth.

Finally, ask, "How will I measure the essays? What is acceptable, preferable, and superior?" This final step involves setting grading criteria, a subject to which we will return.

After thinking through the above steps, write a course description:

This course will be a survey of world history from the beginning to the Reformation, paying particular attention to God's judgment and grace, and the unveiling of the plan of salvation. Student will read *Streams of Civilization Volume I*. At the end of each chapter he will be asked two open-book questions. Selecting one, he will write a one-page, typed answer in correct essay format. Each essay will be worth ten points, five for format, and five for content. Student's essay points will be calculated by adding up his choice of fifteen out of the seventeen scores.

Additionally, student will read his choice of four books by G.A. Henty from an approved list. Upon conclusion, he will write a two-page, typed essay in correct format discussing which parts of the book are accurate, fiction, or based on truth. Each essay will be worth 30 points, ten for format and 20 for content.

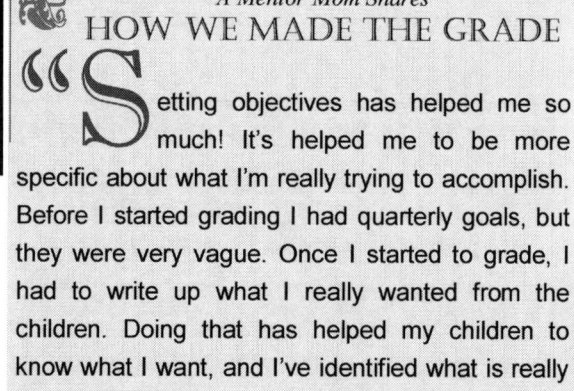

A Mentor Mom Shares
HOW WE MADE THE GRADE

"Setting objectives has helped me so much! It's helped me to be more specific about what I'm really trying to accomplish. Before I started grading I had quarterly goals, but they were very vague. Once I started to grade, I had to write up what I really wanted from the children. Doing that has helped my children to know what I want, and I've identified what is really important to me."

The course grade will be determined by adding all essay points for a possible total of 270. A minimum of 243 points will be required for an A (90%), 216 for a B (80%), and 189 for a C (70%). A score of less than 189 is not acceptable, and the work will need to be repeated.

Alternatively, the resources could be used in other ways. For example, objectives for the textbook might have been

* Compile a notebook listing major events and people. Each event should be described in a short paragraph and noted on a timeline. Major personalities should be described in a one-page report and minor people in a paragraph.
* Score at 80 percent or above on oral or written, teacher-created exams that test the retention of major facts and premises of each chapter.
* Take notes, outlining the major points of each chapter.

These are some possibilities for the historical fiction:

* Create a diorama, poster, or some other display illustrating the book.
* At the end of each novel, perform a dramatic reading of one or more selections.

A creative parent can (and should) think of other expectations for each resource. Since the course is tailored to each child, you have a great deal of freedom when determining objectives which align with your philosophy of education and educational plans.

❧What About Life?

We do not live in an ideal world. Life does not stop just because we homeschool. The sink will still back up and the toilet will overflow. Children will get sick and so will we. The washing machine will break down and the car will refuse to start. Our plans must account for the unexpected.

Sometimes we know the upcoming year will bring unique challenges such as a new baby or toddler, a major home remodel or relocation, or dealing with a chronic illness or incorporating medical therapy into the day. Realistically, this is not the time to plan a teacher-intensive course.

We also need to recognize that many of life's disruptions are completely unexpected. When my mother suddenly died, I could not think for almost two months. Between the shock and the details I had to

attend to, I did not have much left to devote to my children's studies. In another year, my husband underwent unexpected heart bypass surgery. Teaching objectives for that quarter were very simple as we spent many hours caring for him. Instead of only academic plans, we had time to work on character traits such as living selflessly.

On the other hand, in some years we had the opportunity to take unexpected trips or participate in spur-of-the-moment events. If we had rigidly adhered to our plans we would have missed some wonderful learning opportunities.

It takes experience to set realistic objectives, especially in areas we have never taught. However, they are never set in stone. After working with our plan for a quarter we might want to revise it. No problem. We will get better at objective-setting with experience. We might even get to be experts—probably at about the time we finish our homeschool journey!

❧To Make the Grade

We now have all the tools we need to begin an in-depth discussion of grading methods. Once we understand the definitions of each grade or mark and develop a course standard consisting of achievable objectives, we can turn our attention to grading criteria, that is, the difference between one degree and another. It is time to discuss testing, an area familiar to many of us, but in some ways still misunderstood.

A Mentor Mom Shares

HOW WE MADE THE GRADE

"In history this year my daughter was giving me answers, and they were correct answers, but that was it. They were just answers. I was looking for a little bit more. To get an A I was looking for more thought, other than yes or no, and a restatement of the question. So I gave her a C and explained to her, "This is not wrong, but it's not great, not A level work. You just did the bare minimum that I expect. If you want a higher grade, you need to put some thought into your answers.' Then we discussed some of the things she could do. From then on she did beautifully. She picked it up and started getting very thoughtful about her answers and tried hard, rather than doing the bare minimum to be done. That was wonderful."

Bloom's Taxonomy
(As Revised in 2001 by Anderson & Krathwohl)

℘Early Elementary
(Who, What, and When Questions)

1. Remember - recalling information
Student recalls or recognizes information. Memorization.
  Verbs: recognize, list, name, recall, select, state, tell
  Questions: Who was Athaliah?
             Name the planets in the solar system.
             List the major U.S. wars.

2. Understand - comprehend information
Student changes the information into a different symbolic form.
  Verbs: classify, account for, define, explain, outline, summarize, compare
  Questions: Give reasons why Athaliah killed her grandchild.
             Outline the steps a bill goes through before it becomes a law.
             Explain the advantages of homeschooling.

℘Late Elementary or Junior High
(Why and How Questions)

3. Apply - applying information
Student solves a problem using knowledge and generalizations.
  Verbs: apply, construct, organize, relate, solve, utilize, compare
  Questions: Draw a graph using the supplied data.
             Compare and contrast the American War for Independence and the French Revolution.
             How does Deuteronomy 6:4 apply to homeschooling?

4. Analyze - analyzing information
Student separates information into component parts.
  Verbs: check, differentiate, dissect, deduce, examine, infer, reason, simplify, search
  Questions: Simplify the writing process to its five basic steps.
             Dissect the composition looking for the elements of creative writing.
             What do we infer from the statement, "Character counts"?

℘High School
(Is It Right or Wrong Questions)

5. Evaluate - judging
Student makes qualitative and quantitative judgments.
  Verbs: appraise, assess, classify, describe, evaluate, explain, interpret, reject, weigh
  Questions: Decide whether the candidates are qualified to be president.
             Judge the painting using the principles of art.
             Justify President Lincoln's actions at the end of the War Between the States.

6. Create - turning one form of information into another
Student solves a problem by putting information together that requires original, creative thinking.
  Verbs: blend, create, combine, develop, design, effect, form, make, modify, produce, rearrange, revise
  Questions: Create a new song using the tune to "Jesus Loves Me."
             Combine what you have learned in music, drama, speech, or dance, into a creative stage presentation.
             Using the information from the history lesson, write a short fictional history story.

Steps to Form Objectives

ᔥOverall Purpose

Begin with a one- or two-sentence summary or overall statement of purpose for the course. It may be a general or ideal goal or a problem that needs to be solved. Think about what you would like your course to accomplish.

- **Bible:** The goal of this course is to instill in the student a habit of daily Bible reading, study, and memorization. Student will survey the Old Testament.
- **Biology:** This biology course covers anatomy, botany, zoology, cytology, and genetics, with the purpose of acknowledging God as the Creator.
- **American History:** This course is an in-depth, chronological survey of America's history from the time of the explorers to the present.

ᔥResources

List your resources, including textbooks, supplemental books, field trips, projects, labs, or anything else you will use. Designate partial or supplemental use.

- **Bible:** *The Kingdom of God* by Christian Schools International; The Bible, New King James Version
- **Biology:** *Biology—God's Living Creation* by A Beka Book, *Science and the Bible* (selections) by Henry M. Morris, cooperative labs
- **American History:** *The Light and the Glory* and *Sea to Shining Sea* by Peter Marshall Jr. and David Manuel, *Killer Angels* by Michael Shaara, *Gods and Generals* and *Last Full Measure* by Jeff Shaara, and *United State History* (chapters 18-30 only) by A Beka Book.

ᔥNarrow the Statement

Ask yourself how you will accomplish your purpose and how you will use each resource. Answer in several precise sentences to describe each element of the course. Use four steps to form sentences:

1. **Begin with an action verb. Examples:**

analyze	compute	evaluate	list	perform	research
anticipate	contrast	examine	memorize	predict	review
assist	demonstrate	identify	name	present	serve
calculate	describe	improve	narrate	recall	solve
compare	design	investigate	observe	recite	study
compile	develop	label	obtain	recognize	write

2. **Include measurable elements like these:**

time limit	amount (quantity)
length	projects
degree of accuracy (quality)	

3. **Include limitations like these:**

   under the direction of
   on your own
   with or without supervision
   untimed or open book

Verbs to avoid (too general):

appreciate
comprehend
enjoy
grasp
learn
read
understand

4. **Think of how you will evaluate student's work:**

Use tests, methods discussed in Chapter Seven, or specific ideas from the subject discussions in Part Two of this book.

❧Write Precise Statements

Incorporate all of the above into several precise statements:

Bible

- ✶ Read at lease one chapter of the Bible every day.
- ✶ Memorize 15 Bible verses each quarter.
- ✶ Read a chapter from *The Kingdom of God* each week and discuss it with Dad.

Biology

- ✶ Complete *Biology* text reading and take chapter tests.
- ✶ Collect 50 plant specimens.
- ✶ Dissect four animals (earthworm, crayfish, perch, and frog). Prepare lab report including labeled diagrams of major systems.
- ✶ Read selections from *Science and the Bible* and discuss with Mom. Take periodic oral quizzes.
- ✶ Write a report on some teacher-approved aspect of *Science and the Bible.*

American History

- ✶ Read *The Light and the Glory* and *From Sea to Shining Sea*, discuss with Mom, and take chapter tests.
- ✶ Write bi-weekly essays (fifteen total) answering a teacher-supplied question. Open book and notes allowed.
- ✶ Read the three War Between the States novels (*Killer Angels, Gods and Generals,* and *Last Full Measure)*. Write a book report or complete a project (student's choice) for each.
- ✶ Read chapters 18 to 30 in *United State History.* Complete comprehension questions and chapter review. Learn vocabulary and terms. Take chapter tests.
- ✶ Analyze the effects of the New Deal and present findings in a report.

❧Evaluation Example

In subsequent chapters we will discuss various evaluation tools. For now, we will keep it very simple but emphasize how specific objectives contribute to that process. For example, the following could be used to evaluate the Bible course.

Bible

- ✶ Student will receive an A when he reads at least one chapter from the Bible in 10 out of 10 days, B: 9 of 10 days, C: 8 of 10 days, D: 7 of 10 days, F: below 7.
- ✶ Each quarter's verses must be recited word perfect for an A, one error or prompt for a B, two for a C. Three or more errors are not acceptable and student must repeat the recitation.
- ✶ Each day, Dad will question the student to determine how much of the material from *The Kingdom of God* student assimilated and retained and award a grade based on superior, very good, or good retention. For evaluations less than good, Dad will repeat the lesson.

Chapter 6
Testing 1, 2, 3...

When you think of the word "test," what comes to mind? Most likely, an exam consisting of some combination of multiple choice, true or false, matching, or fill-in-the-blank questions. (I will refer to this as the "multiple choice model." I will address essay exams at the end of this chapter.) Further, we usually think of tests in a negative light, something that must be crammed for and endured, but with little lasting value. Constructed so that each question has only one correct answer, the "multiple choice model" test has become the most-used tool for objective grading.

Although the word "test" occurs many times in the Old and New Testaments, never does it refer to multiple choice exams. Additionally, testing rarely occurs in a negative light or as something that can be crammed for and subsequently disregarded. To discuss tests from a Biblical perspective, we need a broader vision.

❧Definition

Test: To compare with a standard; to try; to prove the truth or genuineness of any thing by experiment or by some fixed principle or standard; as, to *test* the soundness of a principle; to *test* the validity of an argument (*Dictionary of the American Language,* 1828 by Noah Webster).

❧Testing From the Bible

The Bible actually begins with a God-ordained test. After creating the heavens and the earth, on the sixth day God created Adam. He supplied Adam with everything he needed—food, intellect, even a helpmeet. He also gave Adam a simple command, a test: Do not eat the fruit of the tree of the knowledge of good and evil. Unfortunately, Adam failed.

In the remainder of the Bible, we find numerous references to tests. By examining some we can learn their purpose (all verses quoted in this chapter are from the NIV):

- ❧ **Tests are for our good:** *Moses said to the people, "Do not be afraid. God has come to test you, so that the fear of God will be with you to keep you from sinning" (Exodus 20:20)*. Also, *He gave you manna to eat in the desert, something your fathers had never known, to humble and to test you so that in the end it might go well with you (Deuteronomy 8:16)*.

- ❧ **Tests determine rewards:** *"I the LORD search the heart and examine the mind, to reward a man according to his conduct, according to what his deeds deserve" (Jeremiah 17:10)*.

- ❧ **Tests teach us obedience:** *Do not conform any longer to the pattern of this world, but be transformed by the renewing of your mind. Then you will be able to test and approve what God's will is—his good, pleasing and perfect will (Romans 12:2)*.

- ❧ **Tests help us to repent:** *Let us examine our ways and test them, and let us return to the LORD (Lamentations 3:40)*.

- ❧ **Tests teach us discernment:** *Examine yourselves to see whether you are in the faith; test yourselves. Do you not realize that Christ Jesus is in you—unless, of course, you fail the test? (2 Corinthians 13:5)*.

❧Incremental Evaluations

Certainly, the Bible discusses testing in terms of success or failure, a grade of "pass" or "fail" so to speak, but what about more specific evaluation? Is there any Biblical warrant to justify the awarding of incremental grades?

Yes, there is. In Matthew 13 we find the Parable of the Sower. After describing several "failures" of seed to produce crops, including those which fell on the rocky areas, those choked by the thorns, and those snatched by the birds, Jesus Christ describes the seed that fell on good soil. When it germinated and came to fruition, it yielded varying amounts.

Still other seed fell on good soil, where it produced a crop—a hundred, sixty or thirty times what was sown (Matthew 13:8).
But the one who received the seed that fell on good soil is the man who hears the word and understands it. He produces a crop, yielding a hundred, sixty or thirty times what was sown (Matthew 13:23).

The ranking of crop yields produces an incremental evaluation of sorts. A yield of thirty times what was sown is good, sixty times is even better, and one hundred fold is the best. We could summarize this ranking by using letter grades of C, B, and A, or evaluations of good, very good, or superior.

The Biblical concept of rewards also supports incremental evaluations. Frequently the Bible speaks of the rewards believers will receive both in heaven and on earth.

> [H]is work will be shown for what it is, because the Day will bring it to light. It will be revealed with fire, and the fire will test the quality of each man's work. If what he has built survives, he will receive his reward. If it is burned up, he will suffer loss; he himself will be saved, but only as one escaping through the flames (I Corinthians 3:13-15).

Although the person illustrated in this passage enters heaven, his reward (his grade) will be less than another's.

Most of us have preconceived, limiting ideas when it comes to tests. By carefully examining what the Bible offers on this subject, we conform our thinking to the Word and experience new freedom and insight.

✋Objections to Tests

Tests, in their true Biblical context, offer numerous benefits. They also have some drawbacks.

Time Consuming to Create

First, although some books come with prepared tests, these do not always meet our course objectives. Tests designed to examine whether or not students have grasped the concepts deemed important take time to create, presenting an obstacle for a homeschool parent with several courses to teach.

Unnecessary

A second objection runs something like this, "I'm with my child every day. Through our discussions I know what he understands and where he needs help. Therefore, I don't need to test him. It's a waste of time." This statement is partially true. However, in some respects discussions *are* tests. Through question, answer, and clarification, we compare what our children know to a standard. If they are confused on some point, we carefully explain it until they understand. Then, we might ask additional questions for confirmation. Jesus used this method in Matthew 16: 13-20.

> When Jesus came into the region of Caesarea Philippi, He asked His disciples, saying, "Who do men say that I, the Son of Man, am?"
> So they said, "Some say John the Baptist, some Elijah, and others Jeremiah or one of the prophets."
> He said to them, "But who do you say that I am?"
> Simon Peter answered and said, "You are

the Christ, the Son of the living God."
> Jesus answered and said to him, "Blessed are you, Simon Bar-Jonah, for flesh and blood has not revealed this to you, but My Father who is in heaven. And I also say to you that you are Peter, and on this rock I will build My church, and the gates of Hades shall not prevail against it. And I will give you the keys of the kingdom of heaven, and whatever you bind on earth will be bound in heaven, and whatever you loose on earth will be loosed in heaven."

Tests do not require pencils.

Little Benefit

Far from unnecessary, tests benefit both you and your child. They show you what your child has mastered and what he still needs to study. However, they also benefit your student. Jesus illustrates this principle in John 6:5-6, when He fed the five thousand.

> When Jesus looked up and saw a great crowd coming toward him, he said to Philip, "Where shall we buy bread for these people to eat?" He asked this only to test him, for he already had in mind what he was going to do.

As God of the universe, Jesus did not ask this question to learn Philip's answer. On the contrary, He knew exactly what Philip would say. Why then did He test him? The test was for Philip and the other disciples' benefit so they would grow in their faith. Philip learned to trust the Bread of Life. Our Lord approaches the subject once again in Mark 8:17-21.

> "Be careful," Jesus warned them. "Watch out for the yeast of the Pharisees and that of Herod."
> They discussed this with one another and said, "It is because we have no bread."
> Aware of their discussion, Jesus asked them: "Why are you talking about having no bread? Do you still not see or understand? Are your hearts hardened? Do you have eyes but fail to see, and ears but fail to hear? And don't you remember? When I broke the five loaves for the five thousand, how many basketfuls of pieces did you pick up?"
> "Twelve," they replied.
> "And when I broke the seven loaves for the four thousand, how many basketfuls of pieces did you pick up?"
> They answered, "Seven."
> He said to them, "Do you still not understand?"

Apparently, it was a hard lesson.

As teachers, we can use tests in the same way as our Lord, for the benefit of our children. Through testing, we learn what they have mastered and what needs more work. Even wrong answers benefit when accompanied with explanation. Not only do our children learn the answer, they also learn to think.

Tests are not the only way to grade. While easy to administer and beneficial, they do have their disadvantages. If you understand these limitations, you will be able to determine the role, if any, testing should play in meeting the objectives you set for each course.

❧Using Tests to Compute Grades

Traditionally, tests have been used to evaluate students because they are objective. That is, on properly constructed tests each question has one answer that is objectively correct or incorrect. Tests are especially useful in math, where computation and reasoning skills lead to one and only one correct answer. English courses, especially those emphasizing mechanics (phonics, vocabulary, spelling, grammar, punctuation, and reading comprehension at the knowledge, comprehension, and application levels of Bloom's Taxonomy), lend themselves to objective testing. Other suitable areas for testing include history and science, when learning factually-based concepts; physical education, when learning rules of a game or names and functions of muscle groups; and music, when learning music theory.

The following discussion includes many different ways tests contribute to grades and course evaluations. I offer these with the hope that you will realize the freedom you have to select your own grading criteria to meet your own course objectives and free you from the notion that you must use someone else's ideas.

A Mentor Mom Shares

HOW WE MADE THE GRADE

"I do use some tests. I generally use tests that have been prepared by others. However, I have discovered that Bob Jones University Press has a CD-ROM called 'Test Builder.' That's what I've used with history. We've made a hybrid history class using the world history tapes from the Teaching Company, and the corresponding material from the Bob Jones textbook. So all I have to do is look at what pages were covered and then make up tests based on those pages. These tests are great because I can figure out what areas I want to cover and then print them out."

❧Grading Scales

First, you must select a grading scale. Grading scales define letter grades based on the percentage of questions answered correctly. The percentage is determined by dividing the number correct by the number possible and multiplying by 100. For example

Total number of questions: 80
Number student answered correctly: 72
Percentage: $72 / 80 = .90 \times 100 = 90\%$

Three popular grading scales (these are repeated in Appendix A) include the following:

Scale One	Scale Two:	Scale Three:
A: 90-100%	A: 93-100%	A: 93-100%
B: 80-89%	B: 86-92%	B: 85-92%
C: 70-79%	C: 77-85%	C: 75-84%
D: 60-69%	D: 70-76%	D: 70-74%
F: Below 60%	F: Below 70%	F: Below 70%

In the above example, the student who earned 90 percent would earn an A using Scale One, and a B using Scales Two or Three.

Other scales account for half grades:

Scale Four:	Scale Five:	Scale Six:
A 95-100%	A 96-100%	A 96-100%
A- 90-94%	A- 93-95%	A- 93-95%
B+ 87-89%	B+ 91-92%	B+ 91-92%
B 83-86%	B 88-90%	B 87-90%
B- 80-82%	B- 86-87%	B- 85-86%
C+ 77-79%	C+ 83-85%	C+ 82-84%
C 73-76%	C 80-82%	C 78-81%
C- 70-72%	C- 77-79%	C+ 75-77%
D+ 67-69%	D+ 75-76%	D+ 73-74%
D 63-66%	D 72-74%	D 71-72%
D- 60-62%	D- 71-70%	D- 70%
F Below 60%	Below 70%	Below 70%

A student earning 90 percent would receive an A- using scale four, and a B+ using Scales Five and Six.

Next, you need to determine how you will use tests in your overall grading scheme. For example, some parents use a combination of quizzes (short "mini" tests) as well as tests to figure grades. They use quizzes for practice only, not counting it towards the grade, or combine several quizzes and give them the same weight as one test. Others use tests but combine them with other criteria, such as one or more of the grading methods discussed in Chapter Seven. Still others, especially those using a mastery approach or just beginning a study, use tests as a diagnostic tool to determine whether course objectives have been met or students need further instruction.

Parents who choose tests to compute all or part of the students' grades use them in one or more of the following ways:

* Weigh each question equally, e.g. one point each
* Give more weight, in terms of points, to difficult or complex questions
* Average all test scores earned during the grading period (quarter, semester, year)
* Discard the lowest score and average the rest
* Give greater weight to the last three tests
* Compute the entire grade by averaging the last three tests
* After the test is corrected, award the student one-half credit for each question he corrects or improves on his own without outside help or reference to study materials
* Allow student to retake the test, or another similar test on the same material
* Deduct one half or one full grade, (or 5 percent or 10 percent), for each retake
* Use tests for practice only and a midterm and final to compute the grade

The above suggestions are not a complete list of all the ways to use tests. Instead, they illustrate the liberty you have to set your own criteria. It is hoped that this criteria will spark other creative ideas as you consider the place of objective tests in your plan.

Subjective Tests

Subjective tests require some evaluation to determine if a question was answered correctly. Typically, instead of just "correct" or "incorrect" options, the quality of the answer is evaluated and awarded points or an appellation such as superior, very good, good, poor, or fail.

We perceive subjective grading to be easier in a traditional school than a homeschool because of the wide variety of answers the class provides. The answers determine a ranking of sorts, useful to compute the grade. Since as homeschool parents you do not have the benefit of a group, you need to give careful thought to what you will accept in an answer.

For example, a younger student asked to orally relate what he has learned about George Washington might be subjectively evaluated in several different ways:

* Compare him to the definitions of "superior" to "fail" as defined in Chapter Four
* Award one point for each fact, insight or interpretation to a maximum of ten, then use a standard grading scale (e.g. 9 = A or 90 percent, 8 = B or 80 percent, 7 = C or 70 percent)
* Award more points to "important" information; for example, relating that Washington was the first president of the United States might earn five points while the information that he had wooden teeth might receive only one.

Perhaps you ask a more specific question concerning George Washington such as, "Explore and list three character traits which equipped George Washington to become a great leader." In a question of this nature, you need to think through what you expect in an answer. Perhaps this question has been discussed and the purpose of the test is recall and retention. If so, you already have a standard. Compare your child's answer to this.

On the other hand, perhaps your student has read from a variety of sources and you wish to test his ability to synthesize information. Rather than one specific answer, you want your child to give an opinion and support his conclusion. His answer might be subjectively evaluated by considering the selection of character traits selected as well as the quality of his arguments.

Tests do not need to be objective to add value to student evaluations. By combining subjective and quantified subjective criteria (see Chapter Four), you might assess your student's progress toward your course objectives. Some objectives can only be measured subjectively.

To Make the Grade

Tests might be used in many ways. By examining what the Bible says about tests and the way God has used them, we enlarge our vision beyond the multiple choice model. Although not without drawbacks, tests offer many options to homeschool parents who seek to evaluate their students against their own previously established course objectives. However, they are not the only way to grade. We will discuss several other methods in Chapter Seven.

Chapter 7
Other Grading Methods

We have already discussed several ways to grade. These include completely objective, where the student's answers are correct or incorrect, and completely subjective, where the student is evaluated against a standard using intuition. In the previous chapter we discussed testing, the most common and well-known method used for evaluation. In this chapter, we will continue the discussion by examining other grading methods. For clarity we will discuss each system in its "pure" form, recognizing that no system is ever "pure." In Part Two of this book, as we discuss individual subjects, we will combine these methods in an eclectic mix.

✎Point System

Description

To use the point system you first list all of the activities your student must complete to finish a course and assign each a point value. The more involved or important tasks earn more points. Then you total the possible points, select a grading scale, and determine the number of points necessary to achieve a particular grade. An example will clarify this method, so we will apply it to a physical education course.

Irish Dance Course Objectives

1. Become proficient in the four soft shoe and three hard shoe beginning Irish dance routines.
2. Learn the history and origin of Irish dance.
3. Build the particular muscle systems designed to be able to safely participate in Irish dance, including warm-up (stretching) and cool down.

Corresponding Points

In the pure point system no partial points could be earned. The student would either earn all of the points or none. In this particular example earning partial points would interfere with course objectives. Since the student must safely exercise the appropriate muscle groups, a student who skipped the warm-up exercises would run the risk of developing shin splints. Therefore she would not meet the objective for that particular class and would not earn any of the 20 possible points. Additionally, the presentation of the history of Irish dance would not be graded. In a pure point system quality is not the issue, so the student would earn 50 points when she completed the project.

Irish Dance Activity	Possible Points
50 points can be earned for each dance when instructor recommends that student perform it in competition (at a feis).	350
50 points can be earned for student's presentation of the history and origin of Irish dance. She may choose her own method of presentation, including oral or written report or a teacher-approved project.	50
Up to 20 points can be earned for each class in which student performs at least 15 minutes of pre-class stretching exercises, 45 minutes of dance instruction, and 10 minutes of cool-down exercises.	600
Total Points Possible A: 900-1000 (90-100%) B: 800-999 (80-89%) C: 700-799 (70-79%) D: Unacceptable. No credit earned.	**1000**

Advantages and Disadvantages

When using the point system you and your student know the expectation and the amount of time necessary to achieve a particular grade. On the other hand, sometimes a student might be satisfied with a lower grade and expend less effort than you would like.

> *A Mentor Mom Shares*
> ## HOW WE MADE THE GRADE
>
> "It's hard to grade courses that I'm not directly responsible for, like theater class or orchestra, or something that my children go out in the community to do. I could write my own criteria, and I do have goals for the course, for having them take it, but someone else teaches it. I might see a performance, or rehearsal, or practice at home, or I might get feedback from the teacher, but I'm not writing grading criteria. The point system might work here."

When to Use

The point system works well for repetitive courses or those requiring practice to achieve proficiency, such as home economics, auto shop, music, physical education, and other hands-on classes. It also can be adapted for exposure or survey classes. For example, to fulfill a requirement for an art course, a student could earn points for each art museum or gallery he visited. After earning an agreed-upon number of points, combined with any other required work, the student would receive credit for the course. The point system does not work as well for courses dependent on content or when the student needs to demonstrate proficiency or mastery.

ᔐMastery of Material

Description

In contrast, another grading method demands that a student thoroughly master course material. Upon completion, when he meets pre-established criteria no matter how long it takes, he earns an A.

To use the mastery method, you would need to define "mastery" in your course description. You also need a way to measure it. For example, if mastery was the goal in a math course and you defined it as 95 percent or more on a unit test, your student would continue studying the math unit, and taking tests, until he scored at or above 95 percent. At that point he could go on to the next math unit.

Advantages and Disadvantages

An obvious advantage with the mastery method is that your student could completely understand the course material. Unfortunately, mastery might take more time than you want to expend, especially if exposure meets your objectives.

When to Use

In reality, mastery is not necessary for all courses. Although it works well for skill-oriented areas such as math, English grammar, and some math-oriented science courses, it does not work as well for more subjective areas such as history or writing. At what point is writing an essay mastered? Even the best writers produce essays of uneven quality depending on the content. Must a student master history? Some spend a lifetime studying a particular culture. For subjects such as these, "mastery" might be hard to define.

Additionally, even in skill areas mastery might not be required for progress. For example, new math concepts can be introduced while practicing those previously learned.

Finally, sometimes you teach courses, such as survey courses, for exposure only to provide a well-rounded education. For instance, a student with no

A Mentor Mom Shares
HOW WE MADE THE GRADE

"Mastery works for lower level courses. Up through junior high I taught mastery courses. In high school most courses are survey courses, although mastery of some math concepts is necessary. You have to know them well enough to do the next chapter. If you don't understand certain algebra concepts, by the end of the book you're going to be dying. In a situation like that I would require mastery, but not much else except, perhaps, piano. There are certain subjects conducive to mastery, but most major academic courses in high school are survey courses."

interest or aptitude in music might prefer a music appreciation course evaluated by the point system, rather than taking the time to master an instrument.

ᔐProficiency

Description

Some courses lend themselves well to evaluation by an outside standard which delineates proficiency, such as a CLEP (College Level Entry Proficiency) test, an AP (Advanced Placement) exam, or an acceptable score on a SAT II (Scholastic Aptitude Achievement) subject exam. They are easy to grade as the exam provides the score. A CLEP test score of "pass" could be recorded as an A, especially since it is considered college-equivalent. An AP score of 4 or 5 could constitute an A, while a 3 could be a B because, once again, the course is college equivalent. Some research would be in order to translate a SAT II subject score into a letter grade, since the scores vary according to the subject.

Advantages and Disadvantages

Colleges like proficiency exams because they validate the homeschool experience. Additionally, your student might spend less time earning the course credits if he already knows the material. On the other hand, some of these courses are very demanding and require substantial preparation.

When to Use

Proficiency works only for the courses for which exams are available and where parents' objectives coincide with those of the test preparers. For more information, research exams available from places such as the College Board (see Appendix B).

❧Narrative

Description
In a narrative evaluation you describe, in words, your student's progress towards the objectives set for the course. These specific evaluations list objectives accomplished, those still in progress, problem areas, and abandoned objectives. An example follows.

Literature Course Objectives
The purpose of this course is to become familiar with the following literary devices: conflict, character, theme, structure, and point of view. Student will do the following:
1. Read each unit and complete exercises from *Fundamentals of English* by Bob Jones Press.
2. Discuss each selection with teacher.
3. Write a grammatically-correct short story utilizing elements learned. A total of five stories will be required.

Narrative Evaluation
Units covered this quarter: Completed conflict and began character.

Objective 1: Superior. Student completed all assigned reading and assignments on time. She was prepared for all discussions. Additionally, on her own initiative, she frequently finished lessons ahead of time when she anticipated scheduling conflicts.

Objective 2: Very good. Discussions were fruitful and enlightening. Many times student had trouble identifying the underlying conflict in the stories, as well as the antagonist and protagonist. She especially had trouble with "Miss Hinch" and "Through the Tunnel." However, by questioning and some simple explanations she could be led to understanding and improved her analysis as the quarter progressed.

Objective 3: Very good for conflict section. In progress for character. Student wrote "On the Way Home." She presented conflict and setting very well. Not only did the reader receive a vivid picture of the story's location, he also was caught by the story's suspense. Although conflict was good, student's characters seemed weak and one-dimensional. She will need to work on this area more in subsequent quarters. Additionally, proof-reading in terms of grammar, spelling, and punctuation continue to present problems.

Advantages and Disadvantages
More specific information can be relayed in a narrative evaluation than in the simple summary a grade provides. In contrast, some parents will find these narrative evaluations very difficult to write. Care must be taken to evaluate how the student has done rather than simply list his assignments. Additionally, narrative evaluations can be one-dimensional: either negative, concentrating more on what needs to improve, or positive, listing strengths only. Unless balanced, narrative evaluations present an incomplete or misleading picture of a student's progress. They need to be concise and complete.

When to Use
Narrative evaluations work well for younger children, especially in skill areas or when you follow a scope and sequence. They also work well for unusual and difficult-to-evaluate courses. In complex courses for older children, narrative evaluations become cumbersome. To properly evaluate these courses, you might find that you need to write too much.

❧Tailored Grading Criteria
Tailored grading criteria carefully delineate objective and/or subjective levels of accomplishment required for an A, B, C, D, or F. Although it is tempting to begin by defining the criteria necessary to achieve an A, it actually is easier to begin with the lowest acceptable grade, usually a C.

According to established definitions, a student earns a C if the minimum course objectives are met but not exceeded. Other synonyms include fair, satisfactory, medium, adequate and acceptable. Examining each of the course objectives, you first need to determine your minimum acceptable requirement, that is, what is absolutely necessary to complete the course.

The next grade, the B, constitutes above average work: very good, fine, accurate, estimable. To determine criteria for a B, you specify what, in addition to the C criteria, you will require for a B.

Reserving the A for the highest level of achievement, for work that is significantly above the minimum, you finally add the superior, remarkable, first rate, or noteworthy criteria your student must accomplish.

For example, one of the intents of a history class might include evaluating a time period or culture using the Bible (Deuteronomy 28-29). After each assignment, the student writes a paragraph examining the culture's obedience or disobedience to God's principles. Tailored grading criteria for this objective might be:

D—Student completes all reading and writes paragraph.

C—Student completes all reading and writes paragraph. She gives one example of culture's obedience or disobedience with general evidence rather than specific examples.

    B—Student completes all reading and writes paragraph. She supports at least one example with specific, referenced evidence.

    A—Student completes all reading and writes paragraph. She supports two or more examples with specific, referenced evidence.

Advantages and Disadvantages

Spelled-out grading criteria tells your student exactly what you expect so he can strive to meet your standard. However, human nature being what it is, he can also settle for a lower grade by choosing to do lower quality work. You should be sure your minimum is truly the minimum acceptable standard. Tailored grading criteria also forces you to create clear and concise objectives as you think through what is important and what is extraneous. These clear statements help you stay focused and spend time where needed.

The major disadvantage to tailored grading criteria is its steep learning curve. It requires much thought and experimentation. However, in reality, you do not need to tailor grading criteria to each individual course. Instead, you will use the same criteria for several courses. For example, if you use publisher-supplied or teacher-created tests, you can probably apply the same grading criteria to several courses. In the same way, discussion criteria might be used to evaluate several courses. The

---

A Mentor Mom Shares

HOW WE MADE THE GRADE

"I have used tailored grading criteria, not for a whole course, but for parts within a course, and discussion is a good example. I've also used it sometimes in composition and in trying to make some subjective things objective, like P.E., flute, French horn, and ministry. It is difficult, but at the same time it ties right in with being able to say, 'These are my goals for the course. This is what an A in this course looks like.' So if you're designing your own course, it does fit nicely, because you know what you have in mind as output or outcome."

---

first time you attempt to compile tailored grading criteria the task will be exacting, but subsequent use will make it easier.

When to Use

Tailored grading criteria work well for almost any subject. Because of its difficulty, you would do well to introduce this method into your grading plan slowly over the course of time.

✍What if My Minimum is an A?

It might be helpful to address an objection generally raised with the tailored grading criteria model of evaluation, but actually applicable to all. What if your minimum acceptable grade for the course is an A?

In this case, actually an adaptation of the mastery method, you would list your objectives for the course and what the student would need to accomplish. If he meets those objectives, he receives an A. But what happens if he does not?

In the true mastery method a student who does not fulfill the course requirements would fail and not receive any credit. Parents need to ask themselves, "If this were to happen, would I really refuse to give my student credit for the course until all of the requirements were fulfilled?"

Some will say yes, and record an "incomplete" on the student's report card or transcript until he satisfies the requirements. If they are never satisfied, they delete the course or award an F.

In other cases, parents lower their expectations. After they realize their students will not meet the requirements, they change them. This might be acceptable in certain circumstances. Through inexperience, for example, parents might set an unrealistic objective. Alternatively, if they relied on a tutor who subsequently became unavailable (through illness or relocation), parents would have no other choice than to change the course requirements.

Often, however, this is not the case. Instead, through lack of diligence, the students do not meet reasonable requirements. Now parents have a quandary. Should they stick to their original plan and award an F, or change the course requirements? If they change the requirements, their minimum grade was not really an A. They might have been better off setting requirements for an A, B, or C at the beginning of the course based on their truly acceptable, rather than ideal, requirements.

Aside from the ethical implications, if parents change grading criteria simply because the students choose not to meet their standard, what kind of a message do they send? The students learns they can put forth their own level of effort and still their parents will reward them.

Mastery works well to evaluate many subject areas. However, it is not without problems. As you set your requirements, consider what you will truly do (as opposed to what you threaten) if your student does not master course requirements. Take the time to consider what you would like to see, but also what you will accept. These might be the same, but then again, they might not.

❧Prepared Rubrics

I have tried not to use educational jargon in our discussion, preferring to explain concepts rather than vocabulary. However, there is no substitute for the word *rubric*. Rubrics closely resemble tailored grading criteria. In these assessment models, teachers identify several criteria, then determine performance levels for each. They rate assignments based on how the student compares to the rubric.

Since this assessment method has gained popularity in recent years, many public and private teachers have developed some useful criteria and expectations for classes they teach. Many share their ideas by posting them on Web sites. You might find these useful.

Additionally, you will find several rubric generators on the Web which allow you to select and customize your own criteria. One (at www.rubistar.4teachers.org) presents more than 30 rubrics possibilities with multiple criteria. For instance, the writing rubric allows you to chose up to 18 different criterion to evaluate a student's writing (writing process, introduction, neatness, focus on assigned topic, organization, spelling and punctuation, accuracy of facts, solution/resolution, creativity, setting, action, dialogue, problem/conflict, requirements, illustrations, title page, characters, and title). Of course, not all of these criteria will apply to each specific writing assignment, so the model allows you to choose the ones you want. Then it gives performance suggestions in each category.

Other teachers share rubrics they have developed for their own classrooms. To evaluate poetry created by an 8th grade class, one teacher developed the rubric at the top of the next column.

You will find many other rubrics in a wide variety of areas on the Internet. To locate them, go to your favorite search engine and type in the phrase "rubric generator."

Advantages and Disadvantages

Rubrics offer the same advantages as tailored grading criteria, except that the initial thinking has already been done for you. On the other hand, you need to ensure that the criteria and performance categories match your own objectives for the course. Adapt categories to meet your needs.

When to Use

As with tailored grading criteria, rubric generators might

Poetry	Novice	Apprentice	Veteran	Master
Ability to Captivate the Reader	Unfocused; author seems unsure of direction (1-2 pts.)	Some focus, but lacks continuity (3-4 pts.)	Well-focused and interests reader throughout (5-6 pts.)	Captivates and involves reader deeply (7-8 pts)
Sensory Images	Difficult to visualize image or emotion (1-2 pts.)	Some use of image, idea, or emotion (3-4 pts.)	Clear use of sensory images to portray ideas or emotions (5-6 pts.)	Vivid, detailed images and intensely felt emotion (7-8 pts)
Use of Language	Imprecise or inappropriate choice of words (1-2 pts.)	Expresses thoughts marginally (3-4 pts.)	Appropriate choice of language (5-6 pts.)	Uses rich and imaginative language (7-8 pts)
Punctuation	Arbitrary punctuation (1-2 pts.)	Some meaningful punctuation (3-4 pts.)	Punctuation meaningful throughout (5-6 pts.)	Punctuation enhances conveyance of thoughts and images (7-8 pts)

From www.interactiveclassroom.com. Article entitled, "Creating Rubrics Through Negotiable Contracting and Assessment" published by ERIC 1997 by Andi Stix, Ed.D., US Department of Education ERIC #TM027246

be used in a variety of subjects whenever they suit your purposes.

❧Portfolios

Portfolios, the final grading method we will discuss, provide an assessment alternative. Portfolios can take a number of forms. Basically, they are collections. Showing samples of your student's best work in one or all subjects, they demonstrate skill progression or skill mastery.

Generally, portfolios fill three-ring binders comprised of several sections based on your course objectives. For example, a basic portfolio for a math class might contain file dividers for sections such as your student's best assignments, tests, and projects. Some courses might warrant large artist's portfolios such as those available at craft stores, audio or video recordings, or folders or boxes of additional work.

Portfolios can document one subject or act as a yearbook or scrapbook to record an entire year or series of years such as junior high or high school. Portfolios should illustrate how your child met the objectives you set for the course. For instance, if you requested reports, your student's portfolio should contain his best compositions. Other possibilities include assignments, tests, samples of artwork, pictures of large projects or posters, records or graphs of fitness achievements, personal responses, lab reports, achievement awards or special recognition, or just about anything you can think of, keeping in mind the purpose for your child's portfolio. It should give a true picture of your child's accomplishments.

Advantages and Disadvantages

Portfolios offer a more complete picture of a student's abilities than the alphabetic or numeric summary a grade provides by actually showing your student's accomplishments. Additionally, they can go beyond what we normally think of as "school" and include non-academic or extra-curricular samples to give a more balanced picture of your student.

Portfolios might present problems in certain situations when you use them as your sole means of assessment. For example, if your student applied for college entry, he would need to make an appointment with an admissions counselor and submit his portfolio for review. Assuming an admissions counselor would be willing to make the time, your student's portfolio would be subject to the counselor's interpretation and approval. Be aware that many colleges will not take the time to examine portfolios, but will require a traditional transcript. If you have identified a few colleges as likely places to which your student will apply, check with them as soon as possible regarding their policies.

When to Use

If you simply want to create a memory of your child's course or year, portfolios will serve you well. They also work well for unusual or highly subjective courses such as art or music. Additionally, if you use portfolios in addition to some other grading method, they provide excellent explanation and supplementation. If you use portfolios as your only means of evaluation, you must be willing to subject them to the approval of another.

❧To Make the Grade

Normally, when parents consider the subject of grading, they do not think beyond tests. In reality, a number of options exist including the point system, mastery, proficiency, narrative, tailored grading criteria, rubrics, and portfolios. Even more options exist when these methods are adapted or combined. It can get complicated. However, these options result in great liberty for homeschool parents who seek to honestly evaluate their children. These evaluations help children find where God has gifted them and how their talents can be used for His glory.

Chapter 8
Putting It All Together

If you read the previous seven chapters, you participated in the discussion of grading as a whole. We talked about evaluation challenges, setting objectives, testing, and several other evaluation methods. In Part Two of this book, we will apply all of this to each of the subjects and show how these tools might be put together in an eclectic, personalized approach to grading.

However, before we move on, we need to come to grips with some pesky issues such as whether to include attitude, effort, and ability in our evaluation criteria, the place of honesty and ethics, and our family's late policy. We also need to examine some practical aspects such as ranking our criteria in terms of importance, discussion as an evaluation tool, and how to keep records and still have time to teach. In other words, before we go on, we need to pause and put it all together.

✒Should We Grade Attitude?

The first issue concerns what place, if any, the student's attitude should have in grade determination. Traditional school teachers will tell us, none. They say grade the result, the accomplishment, rather than attitude. Certainly this position has merit. In a math course, for example, the answer is either right or wrong. It might not make sense to give a student credit for a math problem he answered incorrectly but with a cheerful disposition.

On the other hand, many of us choose to home-school to develop our children's character in addition to academic soundness. We do not separate the two. In that case, might not attitude have its place?

If you decide, yes, it does, you might use one of the following methods to incorporate attitude into your grading criteria.

- **Make it some percentage of the total course grade**. A portion, such as five percent or more, of any course could be determined as follows:

  C: Student participates with some complaints. He refuses additional instruction.

  B: Student participates with willingness. He accepts additional instruction.

  A: Student participates with enthusiasm. Eager to receive additional instruction.

- **Objective plus attitude.** Innovative parents have also added attitude to an otherwise objective or quantified objective set of criteria. My favorite example is from Barbara Shelton's *Senior High: A Home-Designed Form+U+la*. On page v-19, when discussing the difference between an A and a B for a performing arts course, her added requirement is, "Be willing to go out for pie and coffee (or salad and herbal tea) after performances and be seen in public with your parent(s) and actually act like you're having a good time."

- **Grade attitude separately**. Your report cards can contain a space to evaluate character traits or work habits such as diligence or time management. Usually a grade of *outstanding*, *satisfactory* or *needs improvement* is used for this type of evaluation.

At times, students at home might display a less cordial demeanor than those in schools. Peer pressure and a student's view of authority work to the school's advantage. It might help to consider a child's attitude, but in grade determination, it probably should be a relatively small part.

A Mentor Mom Shares
HOW WE MADE THE GRADE

"I occasionally use attitude as part of a class's grading criteria, and driver's training is a good example. One of the criteria I developed is, 'follows instructions attentively.' If that is one of the criteria from the very start, my daughter is less likely to question me when I say, 'Stop!' or 'Watch out!' She's not going to say, 'Mother, stop telling me what to do!' We could have a collision because she displayed a bad attitude. But obeying me right away could save her life. I thought this was so important to driver's training, in particular, that it really needed to be included as part of the grading criteria."

☙Should We Grade Effort?

At times we find it hard to give our children the grade they have earned. Our children have sin natures, just as we do, and sometimes they will have problems with laziness, rebellion, or other unredeeming character traits. Through lack of diligence, or even by design, they might be entitled to a grade we are loathe to give. What then? Each family needs to determine ahead of time how it will respond to this possible occurrence.

At other times, a child might work diligently, but still fall short of your course expectations. A philosophy of the day tells us we must be careful not to damage our child's self-esteem. Sometimes we mistakenly feel we are increasing our children's self-esteem by giving them "good" grades to make them feel good about themselves.

On the other hand, if we tell a child he is excellent in *all* areas, we might mask his gifts. God gave a variety of gifts to His children. While one might be an "eye," another might be a "foot."

If the foot should say, "Because I am not a hand, I am not of the body," is it therefore not of the body? And if the ear should say, "Because I am not an eye, I am not of the body," is it therefore not of the body? If the whole body were an eye, where would be the hearing? If the whole were hearing, where would be the smelling? But now God has set the members, each one of them, in the body just as He pleased (I Corinthians 12:15-18).

A Mentor Mom Shares
HOW WE MADE THE GRADE

"I take into consideration my kids' strengths and weaknesses. I'm probably a bit more lenient with one, especially with her writing, because she really struggles in that area because of a speech/language problem she's had since she was young. Things just don't connect. I give her more time because I realize it is very difficult for her to organize her thoughts and get them on paper. That goes back to the speech/language problem.

"In an area of difficulty, I give more help. It becomes our struggle. Science is not another daughter's thing so it becomes our struggle, her dad's struggle, my struggle, and her struggle to get her through. She earns what she earns, but we definitely do give her more help. I might give her an advantage if she goes into a test and studies very hard. I might say, 'You may have a tiny card to put some of those formulas on.' I might give her a, what do they call that in golf? A handicap. I would give her a little bit of a handicap if she's been struggling. If she's not putting forth the effort, that would be one thing, but when she really studies and still hits bottom, then I give her extra help to try to get her over that problem. But she does get what she's earned."

A Mentor Mom Shares
HOW WE MADE THE GRADE

"If my girls are in a hormonal mood swing and aren't teachable, I ask them to step out of the situation. If we're in the school room, or wherever, they must leave. They might balk at an assignment or express outright rebellion about a whole subject. If they really get frustrated—if I have to take the book away, I will and say, 'OK, we're going to do something else now.' Sometimes I get fireworks: 'I've got to get this done!' 'Well, perhaps, but you're not able to do it now, because you're not willing to be taught. You're not in a frame of mind to learn it, and your feelings are in the way of learning.'

"Once when my daughter was totally out of control emotionally, my response was, 'You need to go dump this on God. You're dumping on me, and being human, it hurts me. It could hurt our relationship, not long term, because I love you no matter what, but it could hurt me. It will hurt Him to hear it in a way, but He can handle it. So please, just go to your room, and stay there until you've calmed down and you've given it all to Him. Then come back and we'll see where we can pick up.' That worked pretty well. It got her to quiet down and think. She went out for awhile; I don't know what she did. Then she came back and did the assignment she had found too difficult. She said, 'Here it is, Mom.' She didn't say, 'See, I can do it,' but that's obviously what she meant."

In some cases grading based on effort has its place such as grading P.E., music practice, and other repetitive tasks. On the other hand, grading strictly by effort could lead to an inaccurate picture of our students' gifts. If we tell them they are equally gifted in all areas, possibly through the grades we award, they might not recognize the talent God has granted. Our children need an accurate picture of their God-given abilities to recognize His call on their lives. Accurate grades help.

❧Should We Grade Ability?

This is a hard one. If a child expends copious effort, but still does not reach course objectives, should he be rewarded with higher grades than he actually earned? Is this acceptable? Is it ethical?

No. However, this should not present a problem, given parents' great liberty to design their own courses. In fact, in a major benefit of homeschooling, we teach at the students' level using a tutorial model.

Additionally, Scripture supports this view. In the parable of the talents, Matthew 25, the master gives three of his servants various talents, *"each according to his ability" (Mt. 25:15).* When he returns, he finds the one who was given five talents earned five more. The master's evaluation: *"Well done, good and faithful servant! You have been faithful with a few things; I will put you in charge of many things. Come and share your master's happiness!" (Mt. 25:21).* That certainly sounds like an A.

The second servant was only given two talents. When the master returned he had earned two more. The master evaluates him, *"Well done, good and faithful servant! You have been faithful with a few things; I will put you in charge of many things. Come and share your master's happiness!" (Mt. 25:23).* Surprisingly, he received an A as well. Only the servant who buried his master's money in the ground received an F.

In this example, each servant's task was personally designed and evaluated. Likewise, parents have freedom to design courses and establish appropriate evaluation criteria suitable for each child. (See also Rev. 22:12: *"Behold, I am coming soon! My reward is with me, and I will give to everyone according to what he has done."*)

❧Ethics

A problem arises when parents custom-design courses and give them misleading titles. For instance, parents might decide a student cannot handle the requirements of a typical high school biology course or the level of work in an average algebra textbook. No problem. They are welcome to tailor the course requirements. However, they must not misrepresent their actions. The term "biology" or "algebra" on a report card or transcript communicates a certain level of achievement. In the interest of communication, parents record grades to translate their homeschool experience into a recognizable format for others in the field of education. This must be honest and ethical. Perhaps a course title such as "Introduction to Biology," "Life Science," "Pre-Algebra," or "Basic Math" might be a better summary and description for the course. Our liberty must be constrained by the bounds of honesty and integrity.

❧Pacing

Your children might have the ability to accomplish the requirements of an average algebra or biology course but need additional time. You may give it. You are not constrained by the time limitations of traditional schools. In your record keeping, you might account for the additional time in several ways. If your high school student needs two years to finish the algebra course, you could award credits as earned, for example 2.5 credits each semester for a ten credit course. When you do not count credits, with younger students, for example, you might call the first year's course Algebra Ia and the second Algebra Ib. Finally, you might hold off recording the course until it is complete. When concluded, record the course on the transcript or report card.

A Mentor Mom Shares
HOW WE MADE THE GRADE

"I have had late policies and I'm going to have a late policy again next year in geometry. In some subjects, like our British Lit co-op and Spanish classes, it's easy to implement late policies, because we have to keep going. If the assignment is not done, I don't have it to grade. If my children get a zero on that assignment, their average plummets. When we get near the end of the quarter, I say, 'OK, I'm calculating grades. Whatever is not here, you're going to get a zero.' That's a great motivator!

"I have dropped my children a grade for late work in the past, but I didn't write it in this year's criteria, partly because I forgot about it and partly because it's very hard to enforce. I just get so sidetracked with the rest of life."

❧Late Policy

Several years ago while attending a homeschool convention, it was my privilege to listen to a speaker from a prestigious college advise parents on college entry requirements. One thing he said hit a chord. When asked how homeschooled students do in college, he said they have a very difficult time meeting deadlines, that is, turning work in on time. He explained, "Without Mom standing behind them, they don't do very well." Ouch!

Unfortunately, this criticism rings true. How often do we extend perfectly reachable deadlines just because our children mismanaged their time? Or perhaps we do not set deadlines at all. Being deficient in time management ourselves, perhaps we neglect to teach this skill to our children. In my own home, I have frequently extended a deadline for, I am sorry to admit, sloppy reasons. What does this teach our children?

When setting up grading criteria, you might want to give thought to your late policy. Will it be strictly enforced or somewhat lenient? Will late assignments be accepted or penalized? How, exactly, is "late" defined? If an assignment is due at 4:30 on a Tuesday, when will it be late? At 4:31? 5:00? Wednesday morning? Give thought to your policy because your children will be sure to ask.

Another consideration: If the assignment is late, then what? Will the grade be affected and if so, how? Late policy examples include the following:

- ❧ No late submissions will be accepted. They will be recorded as a zero.
- ❧ Late submissions will be decreased one (or one half) letter grade.
- ❧ Late submissions will be decreased one (or one half) letter grade for each day they are late.

Students should learn that being on time is the norm. If a student has a real problem in this area, however, positive rewards might be more effective than negative. Consequently, during the time they are working on this trait, some parents have chosen to reward their students for work submitted early by increasing their grade. For example, an assignment due Wednesday which earned a B might earn a B+ if turned in on Tuesday. Whether you choose to use positive or negative rewards, consider the place of time management in your grading criteria.

❧Establishing Weights

Before we look at individual subject areas and possible methods to measure progress, we need to spend just a little more time examining our course objectives. All objectives are not equal. That is, some will be more important to us than others. For example, a science

A Mentor Mom Shares
HOW WE MADE THE GRADE

"Especially as we've gotten into the upper grades, I actually have to think about grading criteria and linking the grades to the goals and how I'm going to weight different parts. That's been a benefit and also a challenge. I wrestle with weighting. In Spanish, how do I weight the oral, versus the written; or in literature, the discussions versus the compositions versus the reading? To try to divide it up and figure out, 'Well is this half the grade, is it a third of the grade?' That sort of thing is difficult for me."

course might include three objectives:

1. Assimilate and retain information from primary references (textbooks or other resources).
2. Conduct five labs and write reports on each.
3. Participate in three field trips.

If an evaluation method were selected for each requirement, a student could receive an A for task one, a C for task two, and a B for task three. Now what? Should these three evaluations be averaged so that the student receives a B for the grade? This would be appropriate if you consider all objectives equal, but not if some were more important than others.

After some thought, you decide task one is most important and should comprise three-quarters of the student's grade. Consequently you assign it a weight of 75 percent. Labs might come second, worth one-fifth of the total, so you give them a 20 percent weight. You think of field trips as supplements or enhancements and allot them only 5 percent of the total. By converting the letter grades into their numeric equivalents (A = 4, B = 3, C = 2, D = 1), and the weight into decimal format (by dividing it by 100), the science grade might be computed as follows:

Goal	Weight	x	Grade	=	Total
Resources	.75 (75%)		4 (A)		3.0
Labs	.20 (20%)		2 (C)		.4
Field Trips	.05 (5%)		3 (B)		.2
Grade					**3.6**

Since 3.6 is equivalent to 90 percent (3.6/4 = .90 x 100 = 90%), the student would earn either an A– or a B, depending on the grading scale (see Appendix A).

The weights assigned to each portion of the grade must correspond to the course objectives. In a hands-on or lab-oriented course, the lab weight would probably increase, while in an experiential course the field trip weight would rise.

✎Evaluating Discussions

Through discussion you learn whether or not your student has met your course objectives; however, assigning a grade offers its own challenges. I will discuss four methods ranging from very simple to complex.

First, tailored criteria could be sketched:

C—Student is prepared for the discussion, having completed all assigned homework. With frequent prompting and explanations, he can be led to an understanding of the concepts covered.

B—Student is prepared for the discussion, having completed all assigned homework. Through questioning, he can be led to an understanding of the concepts covered. He can appreciate and understand the insights and ideas of others.

A—Student is prepared for the discussion, having completed all assigned homework. He shows understanding of the concepts covered and frequently adds his own ideas and insights.

At the end of the grading period, you could either subjectively evaluate your student against the above criteria, or develop a way to keep track of earned grades after each discussion.

Second, you might evaluate discussions with a variation of the narrative approach. You could keep a blank sheet of lined paper near your lesson plans and periodically, or everyday if desired, record a summary of the student's participation. For example,

Date	Response
2/8	After much explanation student understood why the people of Boston felt they had to dump the tea in the bay.
2/15	Student asked no questions. She wasn't prepared for the lesson.
2/22	Student asked especially insightful questions about whether or not the War for Independence met the Bible's description of a "just war." She exhibited good understanding.

At the end of the grading period, you could look over this list and subjectively determine a grade.

A Mentor Mom Shares
HOW WE MADE THE GRADE

"How much we use discussion varies from year to year, but this year history is almost entirely discussion. My children might do some writing, but our history has been primarily reading and discussion. Sometimes I have them tell me back things, not really as full blown a narrative style as you'd find in Charlotte Mason, but something like, 'Tell me what you've learned about the Great Depression.' Then, after I hear that, if they don't give me some details that I'm hoping to hear, I ask them more specific questions; for example, 'What were some programs that were started in FDR's administration to deal with the depression?' Instead of having a written test, we do oral evaluation.

"Science is a heavy course right now. I'm not cutting back in history, but I'm making it more discussion-oriented because of science. I didn't want my children to feel extra pressure while they're putting together their plant and animal taxonomy notebooks. But in other years, for example, when we did California history, then another subject became a little more discussion-oriented so my children could spend more reading, writing, and research time in the history course."

A Mentor Mom Shares
HOW WE MADE THE GRADE

"This last quarter we were doing a kitchen remodel and the younger children were reading *The Red Badge of Courage*. We were supposed to discuss it along the way and I didn't have any time. They finished the book and when we finally sat down to discuss it, they came with notes on each of the questions so they could discuss them with knowledge. That to me right there was an A because they had never done that before. They never had taken the initiative to really think about the questions before they came for a discussion. They had always let me or someone else lead the discussion, jumping in once and a while. I saw real growth that day."

Third, track discussions using symbols. To illustrate:

Symbol	Meaning
∪	Good response
∩	Poor response
!	Insightful response
?	Good question
Ø	No response to a direct question

For most situations, complex criteria, like these symbols, might require too much effort. On the other hand, they could be especially useful to track a group discussion.

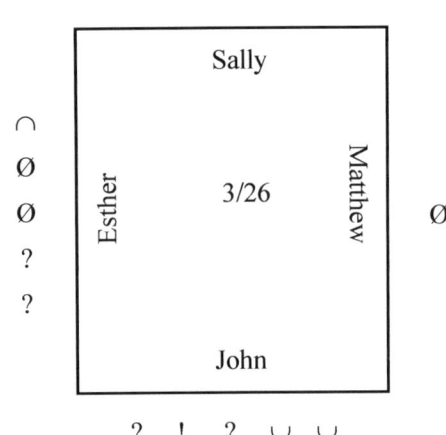

Finally, when setting discussion criteria to determine whether or not your student met your course objectives, be careful to evaluate content. Consider the following:

C—Student participates with some complaints and refuses additional instruction.

B—Student participates with willingness and accepts additional instruction.

A—Student participates with enthusiasm and eagerly receives additional instruction.

These criteria measure attitude more than content. If you wanted to teach or encourage your students to participate in discussions, it would work well; however, to decide how much of the course was absorbed, it lacks as a measurement tool.

✎To Make the Grade

By now it should be very evident how much freedom parents have in which to ethically and honestly evaluate their own children. Of course, some evaluation systems will be more cumbersome than others to implement and maintain. On the other hand, by seeing and understanding these methods, you might be able to adapt them to your needs. Next up—record keeping.

Chapter 9
Record Keeping

Before we continue with the subjects, we need to stop and address an objection. This is pretty complicated. How are homeschool parents with multiple children and subjects supposed to keep track of all this stuff? What kinds of records do we need to keep?

Simple records suffice, especially for younger students. Yes, computer-generated or typed forms look neat and professional, but unless you plan to get multiple uses from your system, it might not be worth the time it takes to create them.

For instance, it might be worthwhile to create a Bible reading log for students to record the date each chapter was read. This might be especially important if one of your Bible objectives includes reading through the entire Bible. Since this task might take several years, you might feel it worth the effort to create a special form.

On the other hand, if the event is a small portion of the course, fancy record-keeping might take too much time. For example, if a history course included just one field trip, it might not make sense to create a special field trip evaluation form.

A maxim called the "law of diminishing marginal utility" states that at some point greater effort does not result in a corresponding increase in benefit. In fact, at its conclusion, greater effort results in a decrease in benefit. Consider the following graph:

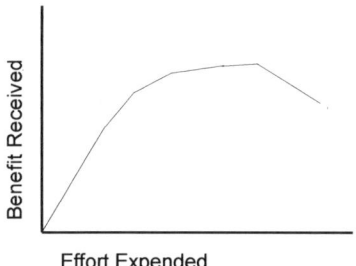

Law of Diminishing Marginal Utility

At the beginning of this graph, increased effort, for example, taking the time to think through evaluation criteria and set up some kind of record-keeping system, resulted in great benefit. However, at some point further tinkering with the system no longer profited. Finally, the system got so complex that rather than benefiting, it detracted from the accomplishment of course objectives. Just when does further effort result in little or decreased benefit? Only the family can say for sure. Balance is necessary. Most of the time, moderate record-keeping suffices.

◈ Record-Keeping For High School

What about high school students? Is special record-keeping required for them? Probably. To answer, you need to consider your children's future plans. Usually students pursue one of four different paths or directions upon graduation from high school.

First, they might discontinue formal education. Upon graduation these students plan to start a business, seek employment, or practice being a keeper-at-home in preparation for marriage. Their school objectives emphasize both academics and life-preparation. Since the parents of these students do not envision giving an account of their students' progress to any outside authority, a college admissions counselor or military recruiter, for example, record-keeping might be more relaxed. In this case the records are for the family's benefit only and should conform to their level of comfort.

Second, students might enter the military, or a business, trade, or vocational school for a short period of training, or complete a two-year vocational program at a junior college before pursuing employment. Many, in fact most, of these organizations will require transcripts listing course titles, credits, and grades achieved, requiring parents to keep records to explain their system.

Third, students might choose to attend a two-year junior college with the idea of earning an Associates in Arts, or equivalent, degree before transferring to a four-year college or university. More involved record-keeping will be required for this student. Although some two-year junior colleges have no entry requirements whatsoever, others require the student to produce a transcript upon application. Additionally, this transcript might be required when the student transfers to a four-year college or university. If the student has done well at the junior college, your transcript will probably be accepted without further documentation. On the other hand, the college might ask for more information, such as course descriptions and grading criteria. In the absence of records, the college might request a conference, some kind of testing, accept the student on probation, or turn him away. You should keep adequate records or be prepared to accept potential consequences of your decision.

Finally, students might apply to enter a four-year college or university after graduation from high school. In a conventional school, these students take "college prep" courses which have been reviewed and approved by colleges. You might use these to model your own courses. Although requirements will vary from college to college, Cathy Duffy (*Christian Home Educators' Manual*) says,

> Many colleges want to know your standards and methods for determining grades so that they can judge how valid they might be." p. 94

> Because colleges often doubt a parent's ability to objectively grade his or her own child, they are sometimes skeptical of home school grade point averages. However, if they do consider a homeschooler's grades, colleges are likely to ask what criteria were used for grading, or how work was objectively evaluated. p. 95

Cedarville College, when discussing its entrance requirements for homeschoolers, says,

> Because curricula vary from one home schooling program to another, it's important for you to provide an explanation of your curriculum and your educator's teaching methods.

>   ✴ Who is ultimately responsible for setting up curriculum and selecting materials?

>   ✴ What type of curriculum and materials did your educator(s) use?

>   ✴ Who was responsible for providing instruction? Did you have tutors in some areas and not in others, etc?

>   ✴ Who recorded your grades and how?

>   ✴ What type of independent, standardized testing was used to measure your progress against a larger population? (Include copies of this information with your transcript.) www.cedarville.edu/dept/adm/1_req.htm

Of the four paths, the student heading to a four-year college will need to have the most complete records. Even when students are unsure of their future plans, the safest course is to plan as if students are going directly to a four-year college, because you never know for certain what your children will do next. If you do not keep proper records, it will be too late to fix the problem in grade 12.

✎Keeping Those Records

Right. So how do we do this and still have time to teach? First of all, some of the record-keeping should be done by your children, especially activities such as keeping track of reading or repetitive activities such as P.E.

Second, some parents require their students to file completed and evaluated work in a notebook devoted to the subject. At the end of the grading period, the parent spends several hours examining the notebooks and calculating grades.

Third, if you already keep a lesson planner or some type of daily or monthly activity report, you could record grades as earned. At the end of the grading period calculate grades using your notes.

Sometimes it is worthwhile to create forms. Although time-consuming, the time might be saved when figuring grades.

✎If You Want to Use Forms...

Since computers, word processing programs, and desktop publishing programs are very common and easy to use, you might spend a few hours at the beginning of the year to design your own forms. In reality, parents find they use very similar criteria from course to course. For example, discussion might be used as a primary evaluation tool in several subjects. Consequently, the same evaluation form might work for several courses. Alternatively, if parents frequently require book reports, it might be worthwhile to create a book report evaluation form and use it in multiple subjects.

A generic chart like the one below might be customized to record a variety of activity.

The columns in the above chart could be filled in and used to track a number of courses such as Bible recitation:

Bible Recitation					
Verse	**Date**	**Number of Errors**			
Luke 2: 1-19	11-3-00	3	2	(1)	0
John 14:1-6	1-19-01	3	2	1	(0)
John 15:1-12	3-30-01	3	2	(1)	0
Matthew 5:1-16	6-8-01	3	(2)	1	0

The chart could also be modified to evaluate a student's piano recital; for example:

Piano Recital				
Area	Poor	Good	Very Good	Superior
Skill	1	2	(3)	4
Expression	1	2	3	(4)
Dynamics	1	2	(3)	4
Phrasing	1	(2)	3	4

A second type of generic chart may be required to record repetitive activities:

For example, to record P.E. activity student would fill in date and hours:

Physical Education Log								
Activity	Date	Hours	Activity	Date	Hours	Activity	Date	Hours
swim	10/2	2	hike	10/3	1	swim	10/4	2
walk	10/8	1	bowl	10/12	1	swim	10/14	2

This kind of chart could also be used to keep track of Bible reading:

Bible Reading Log									
Chapter	Date	Chapter	Date	Chapter	Date	Chapter	Date	Chapter	Date
Mt. 1	9/8	Mt. 2	9/9	Mt. 3	9/10	Mt. 4	9/11	Mt. 5	9/12
Mt. 6	9/13	Mt. 7	9/14	Mt. 8	9/15	Mt. 9	9/16	Mt. 10	9/17

Parents should be able to keep track of most activities using some modification of these two forms. With that in view, full-size, generic forms which may be copied and adapted appear in Appendix C.

✍To Make the Grade

We now turn our attention to specific suggestions for each subject area. In Part Two, we apply many of the ideas we have discussed to specific subject areas. Although varying in details, the procedure follows a specific pattern:

1. Set objectives. The more reachable, specific, and measurable these are, the easier it will be to determine whether or not they have been met.

2. Determine evaluation criteria and set up a tracking system. All of the examples begin simply and become more complex. Parents should compose their own system depending on their course objectives and educational philosophy. Additional considerations include the requirements of an umbrella program or accountability organization, students' abilities, talents, and long-range plans, and parents' own law of diminishing marginal utility.

3. Do it!

In one of the major benefits of homeschooling, we design our course of study to reflect our families' personal philosophy of education. Grading measures and reports how well your children met the goals, plans, and objectives you set for the course. I have said this before: Some of the suggestions here will not fit in with your philosophy. Leave them. Others will work well. Use them. Some will spark other creative ideas of your own. Adapt them. Above all, remember the Lord's admonition to the Galatians.

Stand fast therefore in the liberty wherewith Christ hath made us free, and be not entangled again with the yoke of bondage (Gal. 5:1).

Part Two

Evaluating
the Subjects

*Applying the approaches outlined in Part One to the
individual subject areas.*

Chapter 10
Math Evaluations

When we begin to grade, we usually choose the straight-forward, orderly area of math. We need to approach it in a manner that glorifies the Lord.

> *But the word of the LORD was unto them precept upon precept, precept upon precept; line upon line, line upon line; here a little, and there a little (Isaiah 28:13).*

Nevertheless, we make choices when establishing grading criteria. Since a majority of math materials use a programmed approach, objective tools work well.

❧Assignments

First, consider how will you evaluate assignments. Some parents grade each assignment, total them, and treat the average as another test. Others do not record assignment scores, believing students should have time to practice concepts learned. Instead, they use some combination of the following:

Completed, corrected, and filed
On time
All work shown

For example

C: Assignment completed, corrected, and filed in notebook.

B: Assignment completed on time, corrected, and filed in notebook.

A: Assignment completed on time, corrected, and filed in notebook. All work is shown next to the problem's answer.

Take care when verbalizing your own criteria. If you were to insist that all criteria be met to receive the grade, in this example an assignment completed and corrected on time with all work shown, but not filed, would receive no credit.

❧Testing

Second, will you use tests? If so, will they be open book? Will your student be able to receive half– or full-credit for problems he corrects on his own? Do publishers have suggestions for using their tests? Will you record all test scores or discard the lowest? Will you include a mid-term or final? Will it have more weight than a regular test? Will later tests have more weight than those covering earlier lessons? (See Chapter Six, "Testing 1, 2, 3…") Additionally, you must choose a grading scale like one of those in Appendix A.

❧Put Them Together

Finally, what portion of the grade will be determined by tests and by assignments? Will other factors be included as well? Possibilities include the following:

🞰 Compute test average. If 100 percent of the assignments were completed and corrected, add five percent to test average. If 95 to 99 percent of the assignments were completed and corrected, maintain test average. If less than 95 percent of the assignments were completed and corrected, decrease test average by five percent.

🞰 Chapter tests 50 percent, Mid-term 20 percent and final 30 percent.

🞰 The average of all assignment scores will equal one test score. (For example, if there were five tests in the grading period, the assignments would count the same as a sixth test or 18 percent of the grade. On the other hand, if there were only two tests in

---

A Mentor Mom Shares
HOW WE MADE THE GRADE

"In the middle grades I used the tests that came with the Saxon math books diagnostically at the beginning of the year to determine where to start in the textbook. The books begin by reviewing the previous year and most of the time my children did not need much of that. Every day we did a test until they started missing problems and getting low B's. Then I would look at the particular problems they were missing, and if they were grouped around one concept, I'd think, 'OK, there's something they don't remember or that I didn't do a good job of teaching.' We might stop and work on that. Then I'd test again, and if they'd gotten that concept and were back up in the A's, we'd keep doing those tests. When they started missing certain items consistently and it was obvious they were hitting things they didn't know, that's where we would start in the text."

the grading period, assignments would account for 33 percent of the grade.)

Determine the grade by averaging scores.

When you grade math courses, keep your child's capabilities and long range plans in mind. If your student pursues a "college prep" course he might prepare himself for the way colleges grade math courses, using mid-terms and finals. Students with math difficulties might benefit from a mastery approach and continue to practice new concepts until they achieved 95 percent accuracy (or whatever you determine to be "mastery"). Although you may choose your own grading criteria, your choice should consider your student's future.

Math Projects

Other grading criteria might include projects or application. In a measurement unit the student might apply what he has learned to a construction project such as building a bird house. An older student might balance her checkbook. In a redecorating project, a student might figure the square footage of a room, doors and windows excluded, and then calculate how many gallons of paint to buy if two coats are needed. A creative parent could easily think of many other ways to apply math lessons to situations in the student's life and perhaps include them in the math evaluation.

To Make the Math Grade

When you begin to experiment with grading, begin with math. After some familiarity, you will gain confidence and be ready to tackle the more challenging and complex subjects.

A Mentor Mom Shares
HOW WE MADE THE GRADE

"With math I've used the tests that the textbook provides. Occasionally, I've added extra credit. I've also allowed my children to earn partial credit for corrected problems. If they can work through the problem again and say, 'Oh! That was a dumb mistake!' then I've met my goal of knowing they know how to work the problem. If they've just had an off day or their brain stepped out for a minute on that problem and they can come back and work it, without me, without the text, without the solution manual, they've met my goal. So I give them partial credit back on the test for those corrections."

Chapter 11
Bible Evaluations

Bible courses offer unique evaluation challenges because some objectives we would like our children to achieve fall outside our jurisdiction. (See the discussion in Chapter Four on reachable objectives.) Although worthy, these outcomes are between the child and the Holy Spirit. When setting objectives for Bible courses, we need to avoid those that are internal to the student (e.g. salvation) and concern ourselves with those that are external.

Above all students need to understand

All Scripture is God-breathed and is useful for teaching, rebuking, correcting and training in righteousness (2 Timothy 3:16).
and
For prophecy never had its origin in the will of man, but men spoke from God as they were carried along by the Holy Spirit (2 Peter 1:21).

Objectives will be specifically tailored to match curriculum and family priorities, but typical Bible plans might include the following:

1. Know about God, including His character and work, the effect of sin, and His gift of redemption.
2. Be familiar with the content of the Bible, including its chronology, people, events, and doctrine. Have a basic knowledge of future events.
3. Have a thorough comprehension of the life and chronology of the incarnate Christ, especially the events of the Passion Week (the last week of Christ's life).
4. Apply Biblical knowledge to real life situations.
5. Maintain a consistent time of Bible reading and devotion.
6. Commit large portions of the Word to memory.
7. Understand how to use basic Bible tools such as a dictionary and concordance.

We can combine these objectives into several categories. In the remainder of this chapter, we will discuss how to evaluate each category.

✺Tests and Discussion

Objectives one, two, and three concern facts. They deal with lower level critical thinking skills (see Bloom's Taxonomy, Chapter Five) and lend themselves to objective testing and measurement. To exemplify

✳ Using publisher-supplied or teacher-created

tests, student will earn an A if 90 to 100 percent of the questions are answered correctly, a B for 80 to 89 percent, and a C for 70 to 79 percent. If less than 70 percent of the questions are answered correctly, the lesson will be repeated.

These same objectives might be evaluated more subjectively. For example, you might read a chapter or two from the Bible and/or a commentary, then discuss them. You could gauge your student's retention and comprehension by asking questions. When discussing the character of God (objective one), you could ask your student to list and define several of God's attributes (such as merciful, just, sovereign, omniscient, omnipresent, loving). Alternative criteria might include

✳ Each day the student will be asked a total of five questions from previous days' lessons. If he answers all five correctly he will receive an A, four correct answers will earn a B, and three a C. If student is only able to answer two of the five questions correctly, the lesson will be repeated.

A Mentor Mom Shares
HOW WE MADE THE GRADE

❝**T**he older girls have a Bible course called *The Basic Bible Study* with a lot of questions about their own personal relationship with the Lord. They asked me not to look at it because they wanted to be real truthful and honest. They said, 'If we know you're reading our work, we may not feel that freedom.' So I told them that was fine, if I could just look at it to see that it was completed or if I could see them working on it every day. I have to trust them because I don't want to step between their relationship with the Lord. I was really glad they asked me that because I felt that showed maturity. They truly wanted to write some deep things in their journals. I thought, 'That's great. I want them to do that.'❞

* Periodically the student will be asked to give an oral account of what he has studied. He will be evaluated by the number of details he can relate including specific people, places, and events. Each discussion will earn a rating of "superior," "very good," or "good." Areas which fall below the level of "good" will be redone.

* Each week the student will compose an essay (or paragraph for younger children) in which he summarizes the week's lessons. The essay will be evaluated as follows: Up to ten points will be awarded for the thoroughness of his summary, paying particular attention to details, people, events, and the Biblical message. Nine to ten points would earn an A, eight a B, seven a C, and the lesson would be repeated for six and under.

Since objectives one through three concern facts, any evaluation tool which checks knowledge and retention would work well.

✎Life Application

Evaluating objective four, "Be able to apply Biblical knowledge to real life situations," could present difficulties, but could be accomplished subjectively. In a discussion, or as part of an essay question, you could ask your child to give examples of how the Bible's message could be applied to his own life or culture.

Alternatively, you could accomplish objective four by adding a ministry component to the course; for example, ask your student to volunteer in the church nursery or as a teacher's assistant in a Sunday school. Evaluation criteria could be

C: Student arrives on time for class and leaves at its conclusion. She cheerfully does what is asked of her and has no more than two unexcused absences each semester.

B: Student arrives on time for class and stays to clean up. She cheerfully does what is asked of her, shows some initiative by anticipating what needs to be done, and asks for direction. She has no more than one unexcused absence each semester.

A: Student arrives early for class to help set up and stays to cleanup. She shows initiative by seeing what needs to be accomplished and does it, without being asked. No unexcused absences.

A problem with the above criteria is that they combine several categories. Parents must decide whether all of

Grade	C	B	A
Promptness	Arrives on time and leaves at conclusion	Arrives on time and stays to clean up	Arrives early and stays late to clean up
Initiative	Cheerfully follows directions	Anticipates what needs to be done asks for direction	Sees what needs to be done and does it.
Attendance	Two unexcused absences	One unexcused absence	No unexcused absence

the criteria must be satisfied to receive the grade, or if it will be averaged. To illustrate, look at this criteria in tabular format in the table, which could be used as a rubric (see Chapter Seven), at the top of the next column.

If the student earned a B for promptness (arrived on time and stayed to clean up), an A for initiative (saw what needed to be done and did it), and a C for attendance (two unexcused absences), how would her ministry grade be determined? You could average the three grades and obtain a B. Alternatively you could award the grade based on the minimum accomplishment, in this case a C, especially if your goal was, "to meet all course requirements." You could also assign weights to each category, for example, 10 percent each to promptness and attendance and 80 percent to initiative, then calculate the grade (.10 x 3 (B) + .80 x 4 (A) + .10 x 2 (C) = 3.7 or A-).

Do you have to get this detailed? Definitely not. I only mean to demonstrate a problem you might encounter with highly specific criteria which combines several categories. Rather than combining three factors, you might choose just one:

C: Student cheerfully does what is asked of her.

B: Student shows some initiative by anticipating what needs to be done and asks for direction.

A: Student shows initiative by seeing what needs to be accomplished and does it, without being asked.

Application of Biblical knowledge to real-life situations could also be appraised by watching your child. As the occasion arises you could remember or record anecdotal remarks about how your student applied a Bible lesson.

At the end of the grading period these remarks could be summarized into a short narrative.

Date	Application
4/15	We read Psalm 119 which stated, *"Turn my eyes away from worthless things; preserve my life according to your word."* Today, Debi referenced this verse and said she did not want to see an R-rated movie.

Evaluating application falls right at the edge of our teaching jurisdiction. We want to ensure that our children know how to apply Bible lessons without taking responsibility for their sanctification. Constantly, we need to point them to the power of the Holy Spirit.

✒Prayer and Devotions

The third measurement category concerns objective five which states, "Learn how to pray, and maintain a consistent time of devotion." How can you possibly evaluate this task? Should you require your child to pray out loud and evaluate the quality of his prayers? Hardly. His prayers are between the Lord and him.

Note that the objective says nothing about the content of the child's prayers; rather, it concerns itself with developing devotional consistency. The point system easily evaluates this type of task. A child could earn one point for each day he has his devotion. In a 45-day quarter, a total of 45 points would be possible. If the parent decided that having a devotion at least 90 percent of the time would earn an A, at least 80 percent for a B, and at least 70 percent for a C, a point system could be calculated:

    A: 40-45 points
    B: 36-39 points
    C: 31-35 points
    D: 27-30 points
    F: below 27

Likewise, the Bible reading could be evaluated with points. Pages or chapters could be totaled for the grading period. For example, if a Bible-reading objective were to read the New Testament over the course of a year, the grade could be computed by totaling chapters. For purposes of this example we will choose a different grading standard: a minimum of 93 percent for an A, 86 percent for a B, and 77 percent for a C. Criteria would be:

    A: 83-89 chapters read
    B: 77-82 chapters read
    C: 68-76 chapters read
    D: 62-67 chapters read
    F: below 62

A potential objection to using these criteria to evaluate Bible reading is that they allow the student to read only two-thirds of the New Testament and still receive course credit. If this is acceptable to you, fine. If not, criteria can be adapted by setting time limits:

    A: Student finishes reading all 89 chapters of the New Testament within [the specified time limit].
    B: Student requires up to [one additional week] to complete reading.
    C: Student requires up to [two additional weeks] to complete reading.
    D: Student completes reading, but requires more than [two additional weeks.]
    F: Student does not complete reading.

Parents cannot (and should not) grade the quality of their children's relationship with the Lord. However, helping them develop a consistent time of prayer and familiarity with the Word will produce many future blessings.

A Mentor Mom Shares
HOW WE MADE THE GRADE

"In Bible, my children are required to read the Bible every morning for a set amount of time, 30 minutes, and they are to pray, and they are to do a devotional. If they've done those three things, every day, five days a week, then they receive an A at the end of the quarter."

✒Scripture Memorization

The fourth measurement category concerns objective six, "Commit large portions of the Word to memory." A typical grading method for memory work is

✱ Each recitation of the Bible verse or passage will be worth up to ten points. Student will strive to recite it word perfect. One point will be deducted for each necessary correction or prompt. The resulting score of 9 or 10 will constitute an A, 8 a B, and 7 a C. No credit will be given for a score of 6 or less, and the student must repeat the memorization.

✱ Depending on the length of the passage, something a bit more simple might be
    A: [no] errors
    B: [one] error
    C: [two] errors
    D: [three] errors
    F: more than [three] errors

With single verses, students could be tested at week's end. In a longer recitation, Romans 6 for example, you might test on the whole chapter only once or twice.

❧Bible Tools

The final measurement category is objective seven, "Understand how to use basic Bible tools such as a dictionary and concordance." Although this could be evaluated using objective tools in a similar manner to objectives one, two, and three, especially if you used teaching material that addressed this particular area, it could also be combined with another objective. If the child wrote about or discussed the message of a lesson, he might also define terms using a Bible dictionary, or find supporting verses using a concordance. An additional "Bible tool" evaluation could be derived at the same time the lesson is graded.

❧To Make the Bible Grade

At this point you might say, "This is overwhelming! Do I have to do all of this just to grade Bible?"

No.

We've just taken several years' worth of objectives along with many more evaluation techniques than any one family might have cause to use, and condensed them into three pages. Remember, this is an *idea* book. My purpose is to offer *many* ways to evaluate each subject area. If you find something helpful, by all means take and use it. In fact, if you find one good idea you have done well. You might find the other ideas helpful at another time.

"Can't I just grade Bible subjectively?" you might ask.

Well, of course. As long as you have reachable, measurable, and specific objectives (see Chapter Five, "Setting Course Objectives"), you can measure any class subjectively. When you consider how you will evaluate, your objectives will become more clear.

Remember, it is your homeschool, your calling, and your choice of grading criteria. Do not lose sight of your freedom.

Chapter 12
English, Speech & Literature

Above all, we want children to master the field of English so they can express themselves correctly using written and spoken language.

The field of English includes:

spelling	reading comprehension
grammar	speech
handwriting	literature
vocabulary	writing & composition

Since it encompasses such varied ground, we will discuss English over the next three chapters. This chapter will address the basics (spelling, grammar, vocabulary, and handwriting), along with reading comprehension, speech and literature, while the next two chapters will address writing and composition.

❧The Big Four

Along with math, teachers find it easy to evaluate the basic areas of English because they are so objective. Students spell and define words correctly or incorrectly. They either follow grammar rules or they do not. Letter formation follows the standard or breaks it. You can use any objective method to evaluate these areas. If you use prepared instructional material, a speller or vocabulary book for instance, you could periodically test your child using publisher-supplied materials and evaluate the results using a standard grading scale (see Appendix A).

Take care when using publisher-created tests. They

A Mentor Mom Shares

HOW WE MADE THE GRADE

"I remember when my daughter was doing poorly in spelling. I felt like pulling out my hair because I had tried so many different things to help her. I ended up calling Bob Jones University Press and talked to someone about my daughter's problems. The representative came up with a lot of teaching suggestions. Because my daughter is an auditory learner, the BJUP representative suggested she spell things aloud. That was different. I hadn't thought of that before. We did our spelling tests orally after that and it worked fine, helping my daughter to remember how to spell."

---

should reflect your objectives and test areas you have emphasized. Additionally, they should be at the same level of difficulty as the exercises you have taught. Go ahead and modify any purchased test for your own use.

An evaluation problem arises when parents do not use formal materials to teach the Big Four. Instead, they incorporate these functions along with compositions, book reports or paragraphs, for example. What options exist for them?

Some parents issue a separate grade for the mechanics of a composition. They assign a certain number of points, such as 25, and deduct one to five points for each error (depending on its severity), then calculate the grade. Others keep track of the number of errors, then evaluate subjectively.

Specific methods for evaluating the Big Four along with composition include the following:

* **Spelling:** You want your children to recognize and correct misspelled words. If the word is new to your child, you might teach the correct spelling and require him to record it in a notebook or on a personalized spelling list. If the student has encountered the word before (and presumably should know how to spell it), deduct points from the mechanics portion of his grade. Periodically, you might administer spelling tests chosen from the words on his personalized spelling list. In a particular composition, you might also take the opportunity to focus on spelling. Ask your child to put a check mark over each word he knows is spelled correctly. At the end of the exercise, by checking his own personal list and other methods you designate, he should have a check mark over all words. You could then evaluate the quality of this effort either subjectively or on some scale such as zero errors = A, one = B, two = C, and so on.

* **Grammar:** If your child uses a previously taught grammar or punctuation rule incorrectly, you can deduct points from the mechanics portion of his composition grade. Encourage him to proofread his own paper. To help, notate the sentence in which an error occurs and ask your student to correct it. Or, tell him how many

grammatical errors he has made on each page, then ask him to find and correct them. If your child corrects his work you might choose not to penalize him or to award half of the credit, which he would have lost if he had not made the corrections.

* **Handwriting:** Although formal handwriting books help students learn to form letters, correct usage in writing proves more difficult because students write quickly. The process needs to be automatic. For a child making the transition from manuscript to cursive, insist on legible handwriting. For more proficient students, you can afford to be more picky. You might designate part of the mechanics points (perhaps five out of the 25) to handwriting, then award all five for outstanding handwriting, four for very good, three for good, and so on. Alternatively, you might pick out some letters or words your child needs to practice. For example, if your child has trouble with the letter "w," you might pick out several words from his composition, such as "now," "know," "what," and "knowledge." Ask him to practice writing each five or ten times with good formation. If he turns in this exercise along with his composition, he receives all of the handwriting points.

* **Vocabulary:** While some homeschool parents use specific vocabulary resources, others teach it along with literature or reading comprehension. Vocabulary might be evaluated in compositions two ways. First, check to see if the words your child chooses make sense. Since so many students use spell checkers to proof their work, they need to exercise their vocabulary skills to choose the correct word. Did they mean surly or surely? Shriek or Sheik? There or their? (Once when I was a church secretary, our pastor's sermon was entitled, "The Immortality of Our Lord." He was very grateful when I noticed that he omitted the "t" in "immortality!") Second, you might provide a list of words your child must use in his composition. Pull words from a spelling list, a work of literature, or history or science unit. Evaluate the student on how well he uses them in context. Choose a subjective method or assign points.

Dictation

Another good way to test the Big Four is through dictation. While you dictate or read a sentence, your child writes it down. He must spell all words correctly, include proper punctuation, and exercise legible handwriting. If he makes mistakes, take the teaching opportunity. Periodically, administer "test" sentences that test previously learned spelling and grammar rules. You might also ask your student to diagram the sentence (grammar), define the words (vocabulary), or substitute synonyms (vocabulary again).

In our day, people frequently minimize the importance of correct English. However, if our children do not use language properly, they might be thwarted in their future efforts. When my mother moved to Arizona, she spent months trying to find a job. With no success, she was convinced prospective employers were committing age discrimination. After she passed away, I found her résumé. It contained several mispelled words and grammatical errors. Her résumé detracted from the image she was trying to present. Rather than seeing the compe-tent and talented accountant she was, prospective empolyers saw the mechanical errors. I wish I had offered to proofread that résumé! Mechanics truly matter.

Although prepared materials offers an easy way to objectively evaluate the Big Four of English, you can use these same objective means in self-created exercises or when students practice composition.

ᔨReading Comprehension

Reading comprehension encompasses the following areas:

* Vocabulary—understanding words and their meanings in context
* Finding the main idea
* Sequencing events in the order they occurred
* Summarizing
* Reporting facts
* Making inferences and drawing conclusions

Although abundant resources exist to test, evaluate, and improve reading comprehension, parents might develop their own exercises. For example, after reading a passage you might ask your student five questions designed to test reading comprehension:

1. In this passage, what happened first? Second? Last? (sequencing)
2. What problem does the main character face? (fact)

3. What message is the author trying to communicate? (main idea)
4. Tell me about the story using only one sentence. (summary)
5. In line 43 when the author says, "Laura quickly scudded away," what does "scudded" mean? (vocabulary)

If the child answers all five questions completely, he earns an A, four for a B, and so on. Alternatively, you might assign each question two or more points to allow you to award partial credit if your child answers part of the question correctly or needs a prompt or hint.

Narration

You might also use a technique called *narration* to evaluate reading comprehension. Narration was popularized by Charlotte Mason, a British educator who lived around the turn of the last century. By reading a passage and then "telling it back," either orally or in writing, students demonstrate all of the above reading comprehension skills. Parents ask specific questions such as these:

1. "Sardians to be sold." Who said this? Tell the story. (summarizing)
2. What reasons induced each of the five countries engaged to enter on the Crimean War? Give some account of the war. (facts and inference)
3. How are coral reefs formed? (sequence)

(Questions from *School Education,* Book 3 of *The Original Home Schooling Series* by Charlotte Mason.)

By listening (or reading) for specific content, parents might profitably use narration to evaluate their children's reading comprehension, perhaps using the techniques outlined above. (Note: The topic of narration is also addressed in Chapter 15, "History Evaluations.")

✑Speech

Public speaking is one of the scariest activities known to man, but also one of the most needed. When the Lord asks us to give a reason for the hope that lies within us, sometimes that includes public speaking. How do parents evaluate this area?

If your student wrestles with stage fright, grading might be based entirely on whether or not he makes the speech or presentation. As his courage and experience mount, you might require several speeches. Once he becomes more comfortable, you might want to evaluate your student's content and delivery.

Delivery Evaluation - For example, does he
* begin well, taking his time, or does he rush ahead of his audience?
* use good articulation? Can you understand his words?
* maintain eye contact and interact with the audience?
* avoid annoying mannerisms such as fiddling with his hair or glasses?
* speak loudly and clearly using good projection?
* end well without rushing off stage?
* present a professional image in terms of posture and dress?

Content Evaluation - Additionally, does his speech contain
* a clear introduction to the topic?
* accurate facts, references, and inferences?
* logical flow and forceful arguments?
* good use of evidence?
* good understanding of material?
* a satisfying conclusion?

Depending on your objectives, you might select several of these criteria and assign each a value, perhaps ten points, then award them according to your student's performance. For example, if you choose five criteria, the speech would be worth a maximum of 50 points. Select a grading scale, then calculate how many points will be necessary for each grade. For example, using grading scale two from appendix C, your student would need at least 47 points for an A (50 x 93%), 43 for a B (50 x 86%), etc.

Although parents might evaluate their children subjectively using some or all of the above criteria, they might have more specific objectives. Perhaps a student who has gone beyond the basics of public speaking has problems in a few delivery areas, maintaining eye contact, proper projection, and ending well. To help the student improve, you might emphasize these areas in the student's next speech. Since these are problem areas, parents might note improvement in this manner:

Speech Evaluation				
Delivery Criteria	No improvement	Some improvement	Good improvement	Great improvement
Eye contact		✓		
Voice projection			✓	
Ending well				✓

Any speech materials will offer additional criteria. Use these to develop your personal objectives and expectations for your student's speech exercises.

ᴥLiterature

Literature includes a variety of genres including prose, poetry, novels, biographies, essays, short stories, personal narratives, and dramas, as well as epic and lyric poetry. It employs several techniques such as simile, metaphor, personification, symbol, motif, irony, diction (word choice), and many others. Objectives for literature might include the following:

1. Enjoy works of literature across a broad spectrum.
2. Learn to recognize literary devices.
3. Discern the author's agenda and world view.

The method you use to evaluate literature will depend upon your expectations. These might fall into two categories: mastering previously-introduced concepts and covering new ground. Some of these items might be tested objectively, while others require more subjective means.

For example, if you have previously taught the elements of a short story (exposition, inciting incident, rising action, climax, falling action, and resolution), you might ask your child to identify these in a story. After some practice, administer an oral or written test. Since this is a fairly objective concept, evaluation can be straightforward. Similar elements might include identifying the protagonist (hero), antagonist (villain), conflict, or point of view.

Book Reports

Parents commonly ask their students to write book reports for writing practice and to ensure that the child actually read the books. You might choose from several formats, depending on the age of your child, such as the following two examples.

Book Report Example One:

 ✻ **Introduction** that begins the report, hooks the reader's attention, and identifies the book.
 ✻ **Overview Paragraph** that summarizes the overall plot.
 ✻ **Incident Paragraph** that describes one incident in detail.
 ✻ **Conclusion** which includes the reviewer's recommendation.

Evaluation criteria for this book report might include:

 ✻ **Introduction** - Capture reader's attention and compels him to continue reading the review? All information present?

A Mentor Mom Shares

HOW WE MADE THE GRADE

"This year for world literature I'm having to write my own tests because the curriculum is just literature. We don't have an anthology or textbook. My own tests have both an objective part, usually with literary terms or quotations from works, and an essay portion where students have to write a literary analysis. For the quotes, the students have to identify who said it in the works we've been studying, along with to whom or about whom, or about what situation, or its significance.

I went to an advanced placement workshop in December and the AP classes seem to use quotation tests to get kids familiar with the works so that they can remember quotes or at least come up with a good paraphrase to use as evidence in their AP essays. I thought, 'Well, maybe we better start that now.' So I've started using quotations."

 ✻ **Overview** - Does reviewer provide an actual summary of the book? Is it concise? Does it give enough information without retelling all of the story's details?
 ✻ **Incident** - Is incident described accurately? Is extraneous detail omitted? Are characters introduced and identified?
 ✻ **Conclusion** - Does the review end on an inviting note? Is the reviewer's recommendation clear? Does he give reasons for his conclusions?

Book Report Example Two:

 ✻ **Introduction** identifies the book, author, point of view, genre, and setting.
 ✻ **Characters** are identified in the second paragraph, including the protagonist, antagonist, and other main characters.
 ✻ **Plot** is summarized in paragraph three, including conflict and climax.
 ✻ **Theme** or the author's message is presented in paragraph four with supporting evidence.
 ✻ **Conclusion** discusses how the author communicated with the reader and the

reviewer's recommendation. It ends with a concluding thought.

As with the first book report example, you could evaluate each of these paragraphs individually to determine whether or not your student achieved his book report objectives. Conversely, you might evaluate the report as a whole using the same criteria.

Essay Questions

With respect to literature (or any subject, for that matter), you might evaluate what your child has learned by asking him a question and requiring a written response—a paragraph, a page, or something longer. Sometimes you could require a short, timed response on an essay test, while at other times you might require a multi-page report. To evaluate, make sure your student has addressed two essential points:

1. Did he answer the question?
2. Does he give good reasons and evidence for his conclusions?

Sometimes the question will have only one correct answer. For example, if you ask your students to explain the symbolism of the colors in Poe's *Mask of the Red Death*, you will want your child to list the colors and their meanings. If he misses a color, or forgets a meaning, he has not completely answered the question.

The answer to other questions might be subject to interpretation:

* "Would Billy have gotten his dogs if he had not been willing to work very hard for them? Would he have gotten them if he had not prayed for them? Give reasons for your answers."

     This type of question does not have only one answer. However, the student's choice needs to be supported. If the student answers the question and gives good, compelling reasons for his opinion, he has responded well.

* "How did Grandpa's truth-stretching play a part in Rubin's tragedy?"

     In contrast, this question does not leave much room for the student's opinion; rather, it asks him to make an inference, and relate cause and effect from the story. The student needs to answer the question and identify how one incident lead to another.
     (Above questions from Where the Red Fern Grows *Study Guide by Barbara Blakey, Total Language Plus)*

* "Read I Corinthians 12:12-26. In these verses, the apostle Paul describes how all believers in Christ form a single unit, or body. Think about this description in comparison with Jona's community. How are the two alike? How are they different?"
Question from The Giver Study Guide *by Andrew Clausen, Progeny Press.*

     This question calls for higher thinking skills and requires the student to apply Biblical concepts to a specific situation. When evaluating his response, make sure he addressed both parts of the question (alike and different) as well as gave supporting evidence for his conclusions.

Most essays must be evaluated subjectively based on a combination of the quality of the student's answer, how well he argued his point or points, and how completely he answered the question.

✎All in All

Over the course of time, you might want to put the individual pieces of your English course together to create a highly summarized evaluation. First, determine how much each part will contribute to the whole. For example, in a course comprised of 75 percent English, speech, and literature (with the remaining 25 percent reserved for composition which is addressed in the next two chapters) you might assign weights as follows:

Spelling	5%
Vocabulary	5%
Grammar	10%
Handwriting	5%
Speech	20%
Literature	30%
Composition	25%

Determine the grade for each component by computing averages. If your child took five spelling tests and received the grades A, B+, B-, A-, B, average these to compute his spelling grade (convert each grade to its numeric equivalent, subtotal and divide by five, then turn the number back into the appropriate grade). In this case, the spelling grade is B+. It accounts for five percent of his English grade. (Note: for further discussion on computing weights, please see Chapter Eight, "Putting It All Together.")

If you have already included the Big Four (spelling, vocabulary, grammar, and handwriting) in your student's composition evaluation, your task is simpler. Your weighting scale might look like this:

Speech	20%
Literature	30%
Composition	50%

Finally, when evaluating English, if you issued two separate grades, one for language arts and the other for composition, your weighting scale might look like this:

Speech	20%
Literature	30%
Mechanics	25%
Composition	25%

However you decide to assemble your English grade, make sure it mirrors your teaching objectives. You might not spend too much time on the Big Four with an older student, especially if he has mastered these areas. Consequently, they should be a small part of his grade if they are included at all. Alternatively, these skills might comprise a large portion or even all of a younger student's grade.

❧To Make the English Grade

Although we have a number of options for grading and evaluating English, we are still on comfortable ground because objective criteria serve us well. Most of the time we know if a response is correct or incorrect. Even the more subjective areas of speech and literature might be quantified subjectively.

We lose that comfort when we tackle composition evaluations, which require a more subjective approach. Instead, we tend to grade compositions as if they were English assignments to stay in our comfort zone.

However, even the highly subjective element of writing might be quantified. Since this is a complex subject, we will devote two chapters to its discussion. In the first, we will examine the writing process, or the steps necessary to produce a composition or writing assignment. In the second, we will move on to the product, the composition itself, and give some useful guidelines for evaluating the report, essay, or other work.

❧A Note About Foreign Language

Although we will not devote much time to the evaluation of foreign language, it might be helpful to note that many of the methods used to evaluate English, especially the Big Four, might be applied to foreign languages as well.

Usually, students must learn to write the language. If it is very different from English, Greek for example, handwriting becomes important as the child learns to form the letters. Vocabulary must be memorized as new words are learned. Students must learn to spell these words, incorporating any special characters, "ñ" in Spanish, for instance. As each language has its own grammar, students must learn to conjugate verbs, attach suffixes and prefixes, and conquer any other regular and irregular rules. Thankfully, all of these areas may be objectively evaluated. The only ones which might call for more subjective means might be conversation and pronunciation.

A Mentor Mom Shares

HOW WE MADE THE GRADE

"Make notes to yourself to record grades based on your criteria. Write it down immediately, because you get busy with the rest of your life, and even the next day you might think, 'Now what did she do again? How did she read that Spanish passage?'

"When I'm grading oral Spanish, I have criteria: 'This is how an A sounds, this is how a B sounds, this is how a C sounds,' but I'd better record it right then. That's the kind of activity we're doing every day, and we're doing other things too. It's amazing how fast I forget if I don't record it.

"My oral Spanish criteria is:

A   Smooth, flowing reading or recitation with correct pronunciation.

B   Words generally pronounced correctly but more slowly, the way a beginning reader reads, not as smooth. Each individual word heard, but still with a flow.

C   Individual words heard with more pronunciation errors and no flow.

"The shorter the passages, the smoother the language should be."

Chapter 13
Writing—Evaluating the Process

Without a doubt, homeschool parents wrestle with grading writing more than any other area. We lack confidence in our own abilities. Finding deficiencies in our own education, we feel unprepared to judge our children's efforts. Additionally, we do not understand the teaching steps. We view writing as an art form, something to be "caught," not "taught."

In some respects, this is true. As our children read well-written books, they assimilate the authors' styles and imitate their techniques. However, like all subjects, writing has a set of rudiments students need to master. You can learn these basics, then teach them to your children.

✺How Would You Grade This?

Writing evaluations tend to be highly subjective. Two people can evaluate the same assignment and come to very different conclusions. One might rate it superior while the other only fair. An example will illustrate the subjective nature of writing evaluations:

Johnny writes a report on bees. On his own, without the benefit of discussion, he expounds on how the intricate design of the hive displays the creative glory of God. Johnny explains the roles of the workers, drones, and the queen, examining how all contribute to the effective life of the hive. His remarkable insights display considerable thought and effort. In fact, he completed an outline and three rough drafts before writing his final copy. However, his report has serious problems, including numerous mechanical errors. Although Johnny uses capitals correctly, he makes frequent errors in comma usage and switches between past and present tense. Further, the report has three well-developed paragraphs, but lacks an introduction and conclusion, and uses words excessively, including the word "hive."

Wow!

Parent One looks at this report and says, "Wow! What incredible insight. Sure, the report has several mechanical errors, but in the real world an editor would correct those anyway. This report shows such full content I'm going to award it an A."

So Much Work!

Parent Two agrees, but for different reasons. She says, "Johnny put so much effort into his report. Not only did he spend considerable time organizing his thoughts, he rewrote his draft three times. Surely that effort deserves an A."

Awful!

Parent Three, on the other hand thinks, "Look at all of these mechanical errors. If Johnny doesn't learn to use the English language correctly he will never get ahead in life. This paper deserves an F."

Just OK

Finally, Parent Four reads the paper and thinks, "This report doesn't follow the correct format. There's no beginning or end. Furthermore, it shows very restricted vocabulary. Certainly, Johnny could have eliminated several uses of the word *hive* or substituted *beehive*, *nest*, or even *home* for some of them. I'm going to give this paper a C."

So, who is correct? Which grade does Johnny deserve?

It depends.

✺Evaluation Criteria

What do we need to know to properly evaluate this report? Two things: What Johnny has previously been taught with respect to writing, and the nature of his assignment. We need to know what writing expectations Johnny's teacher set for him, and how far he has journeyed to meet them.

If Johnny answered the question, "What does the organization of the beehive show of the Creator? Give specific examples," he did well. Perhaps he is a young student and this is his first report. Just beginning his grammar instruction, he knows how to use capitals, but not commas or verb tenses. His excellent content, combined with effective use of what he has been taught, would definitely earn him that A.

On the other hand, if the assignment asked Johnny to practice correct grammar and punctuation, and he had ample instruction, his report might well deserve that F.

Perhaps Johnny learned about report forms including introductions and conclusions, as well as techniques to choose strong and active vocabulary. Maybe his assignment clearly directed him to use these techniques as well as a synonym finder or thesaurus to help with word choices. Because of his deficiencies in these areas, he could deserve that C.

Finally, if Johnny was asked, "How do bees communicate with one another?" he missed the mark completely. Insightful comments aside, he did not answer the question. Even if his report were mechanically correct, and followed the form precisely, it would not deserve an A.

In previous chapters, we discussed the necessity for clear and articulate objectives. These are critical in writing. You cannot evaluate writing assignments without clearly stated objectives, but once stated, you can evaluate easily.

✎What, No Arguments?

As an additional benefit, once you and your children understand the expectations for a particular assignment, arguments diminish. For example, perhaps you ask your student to write a report on your state capitol. He complies and spends a week or two on his report. Proudly he presents it. Unfortunately, it discusses architectural features. You wanted the history of the building and its occupants. "This isn't what I expected," you notate, and give the report a C. "But you didn't tell me that," counters your student, correctly, and negotiation ensues. Rather than evaluating using collective bargaining, clearly articulated assignments lead to objective evaluations and peace on earth.

✎Writing Objectives

Writing covers a vast area. At the end of their academic journey, we want our students to

1. Deliver a gracious, edifying, thought-provoking message to the glory of God.
2. Incorporate correct grammar and punctuation in all writing.
3. Learn and use correct paragraph divisions.
4. Incorporate many different stylistic techniques, including a variety of sentence structures and word choices.
5. Learn to research, take notes, and include references.
6. Create moods, emotions, or specific tones to reflect the writer's message.

Additionally, students should practice writing and composition skills in a variety of areas including

- ✸ news articles
- ✸ poems
- ✸ short stories
- ✸ personal narratives
- ✸ letters
- ✸ book reviews
- ✸ essays (persuasive, informative, descriptive)

In general, objective testing is a poor evaluation tool for writing. It might be useful to check mastery of writing vocabulary (e.g. "Explain the difference between a simile and a metaphor") or knowledge of techniques (e.g. "Explain the difference between *showing* and

A Mentor Mom Shares

HOW WE MADE THE GRADE

"I think grading writing is the hardest thing for me, and I struggle with it the most because each person's style is different. Then you have that, 'Well, is this what a sixth grader could write, or an eighth grader, or a ninth grader?' I've ceased looking at what other people can write. I look at what my kids have written in the past and ask, 'Are they progressing?' I'm measuring them more now against their own growth. Is this better than what they gave me last time? Did I have to help them on this?

"At the beginning of the year it seemed like I had to help them through every single paragraph they wrote. Now I'm not helping them. They're coming up with some really good paragraphs and I'm very proud of them. So that kind of helps me, comparing them against what they did at the beginning of the year and considering what they are capable of."

telling"). However, in general, writing demands alternate methods.

Because this is such a broad topic, I am going to break it into two categories. In this chapter we will tackle "Evaluating the Process," and discuss how to evaluate the writing steps. In the next chapter, we will continue with "Evaluating Compositions," and discuss evaluation techniques to rate the writing product.

✎Solomon's Tower

Most contemporary English books offer a set of useful steps to produce any piece of writing, summarized by the acronym "TOWER," which stands for *think, organize, write, evaluate,* and *re-write.* However, King Solomon, a famous author himself, discussed these steps thousands of years earlier:

And moreover, because the Preacher was wise, he still taught the people knowledge; yes, he pondered and sought out and set in order many proverbs (Ecclesiastes 12:9).

As Solomon pondered, he thought; as he sought out, he organized; and as he set in order, he wrote. Since his proverbs were written under the inspiration of the Holy Spirit (2 Peter 1:21), he skipped the evaluate and rewrite steps. With a closed canon, our children cannot claim divine inspiration and will face editing challenges.

Take a look at the acronym TOWER and the content of each step:

T: **Think.** Give careful thought to the assignment and decide what to write. Research if necessary.

O: **Organize.** Order thoughts, usually with an outline.

W: **Write.** Using the outline, put words on the page.

E: **Evaluate.** Proof and edit work and receive instruction for improvement.

R: **Rewrite.** Incorporate suggestions from the "evaluate" step. Repeat the "evaluate" and "rewrite" steps as many times as necessary.

Most writers follow the above process for everything they write. With experience, some steps become familiar and the writer unconsciously incorporates them. Like handwriting, each writer develops his own system and style. But for beginning writers, these steps should be followed again and again until internalized.

When you evaluate the writing process, evaluate each step outlined by TOWER.

ॐ Think

Most parents expect way too much from their younger students and want them to complete the "think" step entirely on their own. This is impossible, an example of an unreachable aim (see Chapter Four). At first, give your student as much help as he needs, leading him through every step. Instead of assigning a report on American history, ask him about his favorite unit. Perhaps he likes the Gold Rush. Probe a bit more. Maybe he wants to write about mining methods, or how the Forty Niners traveled to California, or how James Marshall discovered gold.

After selecting a topic, your young child will need further direction to find resources and take notes. Give it to him. Some parents will object, "If I give my student that much help, it's not his work. He's not writing the report, I am." At first, this sounds valid. But apply this objection to another subject—math, for example. Would you ask your young child to figure how much interest he would earn if he invested $100 for three years at 8 percent interest, compounded annually? Of course not. You would ask this advanced question only after you taught decimals and percents, demonstrated how to calculate interest, and explained the difference between simple and compound interest. Likewise, your children need instruction during the "think" step. The best instruction involves modeling.

On the other hand, once your child has practiced this step, he should not use your brain. He needs to wrestle with the assignment. He will benefit from discussion, kicking around a few ideas, so to speak, but he needs to apply himself as well.

You can grade the "think" step in several ways. After taking into consideration your student's experience and ability, ask questions like these:

- How much effort did the student spend on this step?
- Did he find appropriate resources?
- Did he brainstorm? Draw a cluster chart or narrow the topic? Discuss it with Mom or Dad?
- Did he look for ways to approach the topic in a fresh or interesting way?
- Is his plot believable? Conflict? Obstacles?
- Did he pattern characters after people he know?
- Did he ask for help when needed?

You might evaluate the entire step subjectively. If it helps, you might visualize the criteria you feel is important in a table:

"Think" Step for a Report	Poor	Good	Very Good	Superior
Brainstorm or cluster chart?			✓	
Narrow topic? Discuss it?			✓	
Ask for help?				✓
Find resources?		✓		
Expend effort?			✓	
Approach topic in fresh way?	✓			

Alternatively, you might give your child full credit for just completing the "think" step, especially for a younger student just learning the process.

Finally, you might include *attitude* in your grading criteria. Writing is hard work. Even King Solomon agrees:

And further, my son, be admonished by these. Of making many books there is no end, and much study is wearisome to the flesh (Ecclesiastes 12:12).

You might decide to reward your student's willingness or penalize his rectitude.

❧Organize

Once your student generates thoughts, he needs to organize them. Most children begin with the Roman numeral outline. They articulate main points (the Roman numeral), then sub-points (the A, 1, a, and so on). Again, beginning students need help with this step. You might even have to write the outline yourself the first time or two. Also, instead of the Roman numeral outline, you might introduce other organizational tools such as the key word list, pyramid, paragraph web, topic sentence outline, character sketch or plot synopsis, or other technique suggested by your instructional materials.

If you evaluate this step, you need to consider these points:

* Did my child incorporate his ideas from the "think" step?
* Did he flesh out the topic?
* Are his points clear?
* Is enough detail available to picture characters?
* Are there problems with his story's sequence?

As with "think," you might subjectively evaluate this step as a whole, rate his use of his abilities and experience, and/or consider his attitude and outlook.

❧Write

The third step in the TOWER formula, "write," oddly enough, involves writing. In this step, using his outline, your student simply gets his words on the page. Rather than evaluating the quality of his writing, you need to answer questions like these:

* Does he use his outline as a starting point?
* Does he follow the formatting guidelines you have set (e.g. double space all drafts)?
* Is attitude a problem?
* Does he complete the draft in a timely manner?

Frequently, our children finish writing and proudly present their work to us for review. If one of your objectives is to teach your student to edit his own work, refuse to look at it until he finishes the first part of the next step.

❧Evaluate

Evaluation builds from two sources: your child's own efforts and input received from you. To encourage your student to self-edit, you might ask him to read his work once upon completion, set it aside for one to three days,

then read it again with a fresh mind. Also, since the eyes process faster than the ears and sometimes miss errors, you might suggest that he read it aloud.

Grading criteria for the "evaluate" might address

* Does student himself take the time to evaluate what he has written himself before passing it along to you?
* Does he make an effort to find his own mechanical or logical errors?
* Does he read the paper aloud?
* Is he willing to accept suggestions for improvement?

You might provide an editing checklist of the items your child will be held accountable for in his final composition. This should reflect your writing expectations, and might range from proper use of capitals, indented paragraphs, and topic sentences for a young child, to a clear thesis statement, proper use of footnotes, and logical sequence for an older child. You could also use this checklist as an evaluation tool to make suggestions for improvement. Although you should not expect perfection in your children's work, you should encourage them to locate as many mistakes as they can on their own. The pursuit of perfection frustrates most writers, and will discourage children from further effort.

❧Rewrite

Many writing materials stress the importance of multiple drafts, yet so often our students resist revising their work at all. Rewriting will improve your students' abilities. As I write this, I am on my tenth revision of this book. I've rewritten the beginning chapter eleven times. Although most of the time our students do not have time to rewrite their assignments more than once, to help your student improve, occasionally you might want to create some kind of criteria such as

C: One rewrite
B: Two rewrites
A: Three rewrites

Additionally, he might be reluctant to incorporate your suggestions for improvement. "But I like it that way," he might respond. You student might be encouraged to spend more time on his composition if you incorporate criteria like these:

C: Incorporates some suggestions
B: Incorporates most suggestions
A: Incorporates all suggestions

Finally, attitude and effort really play their part in writing, especially when you evaluate the process. You might want to add something like, "with a good attitude and willing spirit," to some portion of your criteria.

✌TOWER As a Whole

You are at liberty to evaluate the quality of each individual step. Alternatively, you might decide to give your student credit for completing the step. To illustrate, consider these two examples:

Example One Writing Process Evaluation			
	Date Completed	Possible Points	Points Awarded
Think	9-5	20	20
Organize	9-12	20	20
First Draft	9-14	20	20
First Draft Evaluation	9-16	20	20
Second Draft	9-19	20	20
Second Draft Evaluation	9-22	20	0
Final Writing	9-26	20	0
Points Earned: 100			
Minimum score for grade: A: 140 B: 120 C: 100 D: 80			

In this first example, the parent gave her child points for completing each step. This student rewrote and evaluated her report only twice instead of the requested three times. Consequently, she received 100 points which translated into a C.

The second example at the top of the next column illustrates a student reluctant to incorporate suggested improvements. At each step, her parent awarded the points associated with superior, very good, good, or poor. (Points for each category were calculated using a standard grading scale of at least 90 percent for an A, 80 percent for a B, 70 percent for a C, and 60 percent for a D. [Very Good = 20 x 80% = 16]. Since this student earned 70 points, she gets a B.)

Example Two Writing Process Evaluation					
	Date Completed	Possible	Poor 0 points	Good 14 points	Very Good 16 points	Superior 20 points
Think	9-5	20				20
Organize	9-12	20				20
First Draft	9-14	20			16	
Final Writing	9-26	20		14		
Total Points: 70						
Grading Scale —A: 72-80 B: 64-71 C: 56-63 D: less than 48						

Students should know what they need to do to improve their writing grade. There should be no mystery. Although these two examples make that abundantly clear, you might also use more subjective criteria, while explaining your reasoning.

✌To Make the Writing Process Grade

Many homeschool parents struggle with evaluating the writing process because they do not know the process. At one time I fell into that category. I did not learn the basics of writing until I was an adult. Thankfully, we have the choice of abundant materials so we can learn along with out students. I would recommend the *Write Source* series of handbooks, as they provide a good overview of the writing process. Several books are available for various grade levels.

Remember, a good teacher has a teachable heart. You can learn the writing steps, teach them to your children, then evaluate them on what they have been taught. When we homeschool, we have the opportunity to teach two generations. Isn't it satisfying to overcome our own deficiencies while we teach our children?

Chapter 14
Writing—Evaluating Compositions

I suspect some of you have joined us here without reading the first part of this book. Welcome—but before you continue, please, take a minute to go back and review Part One. Without that understanding, you will find this chapter hard to follow.

In the previous chapter we discussed grading the writing process using the acronym TOWER. At some point, however, you will want to evaluate the result, your student's assignment, which is the focus of this chapter.

Writing takes on added importance for Christians. Jesus Christ will not be exalted by non-Christians. We need to equip our children to spread His Word. Through our writing, we encourage and teach others to lead Godly lives. Writing allows us to give a reason for the hope that lies within. It equips our children to be tomorrow's leaders.

God considers writing important.

1. **He wrote:** *And when He had made an end of speaking with him on Mount Sinai, He gave Moses two tablets of the Testimony, tablets of stone, written with the finger of God (Exodus 31:18).*

2. **He also commanded others to write:** *You shall write them on the doorposts of your house and on your gates (Deut. 6:9).*

3. **He uses writing to instruct:** *For whatever things were written before were written for our learning, that we through the patience and comfort of the Scriptures might have hope (Romans 15:4).*

Yet, evaluation presents problems for homeschoolers. Many of us feel unqualified. By breaking writing into smaller pieces and examining each component, I hope to take the mystery out of writing evaluations. Very simply, to evaluate writing, we need to

1. Understand the role of the five writing elements (discussed below) and set objectives in each area.

2. Evaluate students only on what they have been taught.

❧Writing Elements

What makes a good report? Poem? Story? How do you determine quality? With such a wide field, you might think you need many different grading standards. Surprisingly, all writing objectives fit within five areas:

* **Form:** sometimes called structure, organization, or format

* **Content:** God-honoring subject matter or message

* **Style:** word use, sentence structures, and literary techniques which make the writing interesting and lively

* **Mechanics:** correct use of the English language

* **Overall Effectiveness:** everything working together to produce the desired effect, tone, mood, or persuasion

To understand these elements, pretend you travel out-of-state, rent a car, and visit the sights. Sometimes you drive on highways, while other times you travel city streets or country roads. The road system is *form*. Although the roads might be paved or unpaved, rough or smooth, most have signs, at least two lanes, and expect you to drive on the right.

As you drive, you encounter a variety of scenery, perhaps a busy city or a churning, windswept ocean. The sights are *content*. What you see depends on where you travel.

Of course, your choice of vehicle contributes to the comfort of your journey. A compact car or luxury sedan both will get to your destination but in different *style*.

Operating according to a set of rules, or *mechanics*, each car expects you to turn the key in the ignition, fill the fuel tank with gas, and move the steering wheel to turn.

Finally, all these must work together to produce a desired *effect*. A climb up a treacherous mountain pass in a run-down jalopy to share the Gospel with a poor village underscores urgency and commitment. Likewise, a visit to an ailing relative in a luxurious Mercedes over picturesque countryside might make you reflect on the fleeting nature of material possessions.

In the same way, these five elements work together in every piece of writing. Form gives familiarity, a set of pegs so to speak, upon which to hang ideas. Or as King Solomon puts it:

The words of the wise are like goads, and the words of scholars are like well-driven nails, given by one Shepherd (Ecclesiastes 12:11).

Content, the message, might be presented dryly or with vigorous style, both of which need to be technically correct. Solomon notes:

The Preacher sought to find acceptable words; and what was written was upright—words of truth (Ecclesiastes 12:10).

Good writers use all of these elements to produce a desired effect and move us to action. You can grade your child's writing by breaking it down into smaller parts and evaluating each individually.

Big warning: In the following discussion, I am going to get technical. Writing might be hard for you. If you find writing difficult, you will probably find grading writing even more difficult. Although you will benefit from the following discussion, you should also take courage and follow your instincts. When reading your student's work, ask yourself questions such as these:

- ⚹ Does this sound right?
- ⚹ Does it make sense?
- ⚹ Does it flow smoothly?
- ⚹ Does it begin and end well?
- ⚹ Does the beginning make me want to keep reading?
- ⚹ Does the conclusion leave you satisfied?
- ⚹ Does the report support its claim?
- ⚹ Is the story believable?
- ⚹ Where can it improve?

If you read, you probably have developed a good ear. You probably recognize good writing. Go ahead and evaluate your student subjectively. If, however, you want to explore more options or understand various writing components, read on!

ᨠForm

Experienced drivers easily take in sights even while cruising unfamiliar roads. However, if you drive in England, you will miss a lot while you learn to drive on the left side of the street. Concentrating on form, you would miss content. In the same way, readers expect writing to follow an established path and structure thoughts in familiar ways. Although invisible, organization helps readers stay on track and concentrate on the message rather than the delivery.

Paragraphs

Writers build form with paragraphs. Your child cannot move on to other structures such as reports, stories and articles until he learns to write effective paragraphs. Give your student ample opportunity to practice writing paragraphs. When it comes time to evaluate, you might consider

- ⚹ first line indented
- ⚹ topic sentence present
- ⚹ all sentences in the paragraph relate to the topic sentence
- ⚹ sentences form a logical sequence
- ⚹ clincher or transition sentence present
- ⚹ interesting title

Once familiar with paragraph structure, students can

Writing Forms

Letters—Contain personal and return addresses, date, salutation, body, closing, and signature.

Reports and Essays—All have introductions which state the report topic or question to be answered, one or more paragraphs which support and develop the topic or answer the question, and a conclusion which brings the report to a close. Various kinds of essays and reports include persuasive, informative, descriptive, and narrative.

Research Papers—Although similar to reports and essays, research or library papers tend to be longer and more detailed. They usually have a thesis statement (a topic sentence for the entire report or position to be proved), introductory and concluding sections, and numerous supporting points with references and citations.

Book Reports—These usually include an introduction with book identification details and setting, then supporting paragraphs for character analysis, plot summary, theme discussion, and recommendation.

Poetry—Poetry takes many forms. For example, a sonnet consists of 14 lines of iambic pentameter, asks a question at the beginning, and answers it in the end. Each Haiku line has a set number of syllables: five in the first, seven in the second, and five in the third. Haiku does not rhyme and uses nature to make a statement.

Short Story—Short stories and novels contain at least six elements.

- ⚹ **Setting** gives the reader a mental picture of the story's location, time period, and surroundings.
- ⚹ **Characters** live in a story. Authors must make them real and believable.
- ⚹ **Plot** or storyline begins with conflict and obstacles and continues until the problem is solved.
- ⚹ **Climax** leads the reader to the peak of excitement.
- ⚹ **Resolution** follows the climax, winds down the action, and ties up loose ends.
- ⚹ **Theme** weaves in the author's agenda or purpose. While some short stories entertain, others communicate a message.

Newspaper Article—gives salient details immediately (who, what, where, why, when, and how), and incrementally adds and expands on items in subsequent paragraphs.

move on to other forms of writing (see sidebar p. 74).

To evaluate form, list the elements you want your children to include (set objectives), then rate them on whether or how well they met them. A good writing resource will help you create expectations concerning structure.

Perhaps you want to teach ways to write an introduction to a report. Your instructional materials suggest three ways: Ask a question, begin with a quote, or make a startling statement. As part of your objective for organization, you ask your child to use one of these techniques in her report. She writes:

Do you know Patty Reed? She had a doll named Dolly. Dolly comforted Patty during the long, harsh winter her family was stranded at Donner Lake.

When evaluating beginning students like the one above, you might use an adaptation of the point system. Assign each form element a point value. If the student includes the element, she gets the points. Since this student introduced her report with a question, she met the objective.

If you were to evaluate a more experienced student writing a short story, you might include quality. Set your objectives, then evaluate each one:

Short Story Form Evaluation

	Poor	Fair	Good	Very Good	Superior
Setting (Vivid picture of time and place?)			✓		
Characters (Act real? Believable? Appropriate dialogue? Fully developed?)					✓
Plot (Engaging conflict, believable obstacles?)				✓	
Climax (Exciting? Dramatic? Entices reader to continue?)				✓	
Resolution (Satisfying? All loose ends tied up?)					✓
Theme (Apparent? Entertainment? Agenda? Godly?)				✓	

You would not have to use a chart like the above, but you would need to spend some time thinking about what you want your child to produce. Of course, you would want to communicate these expectations to her as well.

Additionally, consider how you will turn your evaluation into a grade. In the above evaluation, would you average all of the criteria and award a grade of "very good," or would you require a minimum level for all elements and rate the student "good"?

Additional considerations when evaluating form might include the following:

* Good placement of details
* Strong transitions
* Smooth, easy pace
* Builds tension
* Is invisible; that is, reader is unaware of the form

Although bland, form holds the composition together. Because of their training, readers expect compositions to follow certain patterns. If they do not, confused readers cease reading. Students need to master form so it does not detract from content.

A Mentor Mom Shares

HOW WE MADE THE GRADE

"I'm not that good at lining out criteria, but I did start at the beginning of the year with a book [*Format Writing* by Jensen] that explained how to write different types of paragraphs. It listed steps and the things that were expected in the paragraph. We practiced that the first half of the year, really concentrating on trying those different paragraphs.

"After a semester of that, the rest of the paragraphs my children did on their own, without a formal model. I looked for good introductory sentences and conclusions and flow. My students knew the steps, they just needed practice.

"My oldest daughter finished *Wordsmith Craftsman* this year. That was a wonderful book because it really laid out what you needed in four or five different types of essays. I hate to say it, but I don't have a formal evaluation method for writing. I think, 'Did she make her point? Was it actually a persuasive essay, or not?' I look at the book and then I compare what she's written to see if it follows a correct model. Then I add in the overall form, the sentence structure, flow and grammar."

❧Content

Content embraces subject and message. If your student writes a persuasive essay, content includes his evidence and arguments. If you ask a specific question, content takes in the completeness of his answer. If he constructs an informative report, content includes specific details.

A Christian's writing should reflect a Biblical world view. Even a letter of complaint should be gracious. Additionally, students' interpretations should be checked against the Bible. If a student were to analyze some historical situation in terms of its ethical implications, his criteria, or what he used to judge the event, should be derived from the Bible. In works of fiction, justice should be upheld, evil should not be rewarded, and sin should not be enticing. Christian students need to recognize that their writing should always glorify the Lord Jesus Christ.

Additional factors to consider when evaluating content are how well the writing included these items:

- ✻ Answers the posed question
- ✻ Is interesting, clear, and well-focused
- ✻ Displays knowledge of the subject
- ✻ Uses rich details
- ✻ Uses evidence and precise information
- ✻ Cites quotations
- ✻ Analyzes opposing positions
- ✻ Shows imagination, especially in the case of short stories or poetry

Many times you will look for specific information. Let your child know what you expect. For example, you might ask him to summarize a chapter in a textbook. You will help him by spelling out a detailed assignment:

Summarize the contents of *America, Land I Love,* chapter 6 "War for Independence." Your report should contain sentence summaries of all major personalities, an overview of the events leading to the war, the role of the Declaration of Independence, summaries of major battles, and the war's conclusion.

To evaluate, check your child's report against the above criteria.

Alternatively, rather than specifically stating what the summary should contain, you could ask:

Summarize the contents of chapter 6. Pay particular attention to major headings.

Then compare the student's work to chapter headings.

Humor lightens controversial subjects and encourages people to change their view. It especially helps in the area of content when exhorting or challenging perspectives. To help your student incorporate humor, you could give him an assignment such as

---

A Mentor Mom Shares

HOW WE MADE THE GRADE

"I use the Institute for Excellence in Writing guidelines for composition. I really like them because they make my children's writing so understandable and straightforward. The guidelines ask students to include a variety of sentence openers and constructions, use vivid verbs, quality adjectives, and use other techniques called *dress-ups* and *decorations*. Not only have my children learned to make their writing better, grading is a breeze. If the techniques are present and they make sense, my children earn the points.

"For example, in a certain assignment, I might request all six sentence openers, one dress-up, and one decoration. If all are present, I award an A. If one is missing, the assignment gets a B, and so on. My children's writing has improved so much since we started using this program. I'm really glad, because writing is difficult for me."

"Write an article and make me laugh." Content evaluation criteria could be

A: I read the assignment when I was alone and I laughed out loud
B: I chuckled
C: I smiled

As with all assignments, the more time you take to state its purpose, the easier it will be to evaluate, especially in the area of content.

❧Style

Style involves expression. Form might be explicitly followed and content might be edifying, but the writing might be dull, lifeless, and flat. Style includes word choices such as concrete nouns (*judge* instead of *man*), lively verbs (*sauntered* instead of *walked*), and descriptive adjectives or adverbs (*stunning* instead of *pretty).* Sentences should follow other constructions as well as subject-verb-object ("The girl ran home") and vary in length. Writing resources will suggest techniques such as repetition, parallelism, similes, metaphors, alliteration, and showing not telling ("The dog tucked his tail and ran," instead of, "The dog was afraid").

Additionally, style includes writing voice (formal, informal, first person, colloquial). Although first-person narrative (I, me, my) works well in a letter, journal entry, or narrative essay, it would be out of place in a newspaper article. Slang might work well as dialogue in a short story but not in a research report.

Style Evaluation Example

To evaluate the style of a composition, consider the following points:

1. List the techniques you want to see in your student's writing, then award one point for each use. For example, a child learning six different ways to construct sentences might be asked to use all six in a paragraph. The following example follows the Institute for Excellence in Writing guidelines for sentence openers: (1) subject (2) preposition, (3) "ly" word (adverb) (4) "ing," or "ed," (participle) (5) clausal (since, although, if, when, while) and (6) very short sentence (five words or less).

   "(4) Nestled low in Scotland, the Lock Ness holds a legendary appeal. (1) The Loch Ness, a huge lake in northern Scotland, possibly contains Nessie, the Loch Ness Monster, whom people have claimed to have spotted. (2) In the sixth century Nessie was sighted by St. Columbia, who came upon the burial of a man bitten to death by a monster. (1) St. Columbia later observed the monster himself. (5) Although the recorded sighting of Nessie dates back to 565, she has been seen throughout the years. (3) Unfortunately, the legend of the Loch Ness might be the result of a harmless joke. (6) She could be a hoax."

   Since this student correctly used all six sentence constructions, she earned all six points for this portion of her evaluation.

2. As you teach stylistic techniques, as a result of a formal course or as a response to the student's previous compositions develop a style evaluation sheet like the one at the top of the next column.

Criteria like these not only evaluate, they also help students proofread their own work.

Instead of concentrating on style in general, in the category of "words," for example, you could get even more specific. If you wanted to encourage students to use vivid verbs, you might disallow any form of "to be" (is, are, am, was, were, be, being, been). You could subtract points if the student used passive voice ("Sandy feels she is wronged") or add them for active voice ("Sandy feels wronged").

Writing must be interesting. Through style your child can capture attention and communicate his message. How do you teach these techniques? Most English instructional materials, especially those devoted to writing, present numerous options. Use these suggestions to build your own stylistic objectives.

Sample Style Evaluation					
	Poor	Fair	Good	Very Good	Superior
Voice: (Fits composition: formal, informal, first person, honest, natural, expressive, appealing, invites reading)				✓	
Sentence constructions: (fluid, poetic or musical in sound, interesting word patterns, good phrasing)					✓
Words: (specific, concrete nouns, action verbs, descriptive adjectives and adverbs, strong imagery, similes/metaphors, natural)			✓		

∽Mechanics

Mechanics, the correct use of the English language, includes spelling, punctuation, grammar, appropriate word choices (there and their), and citation conventions (footnotes). Additionally, it can take in formatting considerations such as font size, spacing and indentation requirements, title, and labeling (name and date).

Evaluate mechanics objectively by observing how your child correctly or incorrectly uses language. However, remember the writing evaluation maxim: Hold students responsible only for the rules they have been taught.

Here are several evaluation methods:

1. Assign a certain number of points for mechanics, say 25, and deduct one point for each error in a concept the student has been taught. Grade by dividing the number of points earned by the total points (then multiply by 100) and compare to a selected grading scale. For example, a report with five mechanical errors would earn 80 percent, a B or C depending on the grading scale.

2. List areas your child must practice, and assign each an evaluation. To visualize, look at the chart on the next page.

   As new rules are learned, add them to your list. Your child might use this chart as a checklist to improve his writing.

   A question might arise, "What if I've never formally taught grammar and punctuation and want to use my child's compositions to see where he needs further instruction?" A chart similar to the one above might work especially well for you. Identify problem areas and teach the rules. When you believe your child understands them, add them to the chart and look for correct usage in future assignments.

3. Place an "X" at the end of each sentence in which a mechanical error occurs. Allow your child to find and correct it on his own (perhaps using an English handbook, if necessary). If he corrects it, he receives full credit; if not, he might be subjectively evaluated on the number of errors.

4. Use a prepared evaluation checklist. My favorite appears in Teresa Moon's book *Evaluating for Excellence* and is entitled, "Writing Mechanics & Punctuation."

Contrary to today's postmodern perspective, mechanics matter. An interesting or edifying article which contains numerous errors not only distracts the reader, it presents a poor testimony for one writing to the glory of God.

Mechanics Evaluation					
	Poor	Fair	Good	Great	Superior
Capitalization			✓		
Subject-verb agreement (plural subject, plural verb)				✓	
Pronoun-antecedent agreement (boys = them, boy = him)			✓		
Proper word usage					✓
Correct abbreviations (e.g. Mrs., Dr., Rev.)				✓	

✍Overall Effectiveness

Overall effectiveness, sometimes called expression, includes the writing's tone, spirit and character. It combines the use of form, content, style, and mechanics. A composition might adhere to form perfectly, use effective content and style, and contain no grammatical errors, but still be tedious and stilted. Overall effectiveness concerns how all elements work together to create an impression in the mind of the reader. To evaluate effectiveness, ask

- ✷ Does the composition do what it sets out to do?

- ✷ Does it entertain, convince, or evoke a particular mood or emotion?

- ✷ Does the reader feel significantly taught?

- ✷ Does it show competency, originality of thought, or creativity?

- ✷ Does the writing invite re-reading?

Overall effectiveness separates a good composition from the truly great.

✍Putting Them Together

Although the preceding discussion of writing elements got fairly technical, perhaps overwhelming to some, you need to ask this: Is complex grading criteria needed? Do you have to devise grading criteria for every type of composition?

Of course not. Nor do you when you teach the skills. You may always evaluate subjectively against a standard. You may use a number of less-involved, holistic ways to evaluate your children's writing.

You could subjectively evaluate your children's work, for example, using these criteria found on numerous Web sites:

A: Superior paper in nearly all respects. Work exceeded expectations.

B: Solid paper in most respects. All expectations met.

C: The paper adequately responds to the topic. Minimum requirements met.

D: The paper does not adequately respond to the topic and lacks one or more requirements.

Or, for something more complex, describe your expectations for each grade category, then compare your students' results to your model. The following could be used for advanced essays:

A: The essay presents a main idea in an original and interesting way, displaying unusual insight. Ideas are presented clearly, with a strong introduction and satisfying conclusion. Thorough research is evident and points are well supported. Sentences are varied and imaginative in style. Very few mechanical errors.

B: The essay presents a main idea in an original, careful, and interesting way. Ideas are presented clearly, with a purposeful introduction and conclusion. Good research is evident and points are supported. Sentences are clear and correct in style. Some mechanical errors.

C: The essay presents a main idea, but it is uninteresting or general. Ideas are presented with a competent introduction and conclusion. Adequate research to support points is evident. Sentences are correct, but flat in tone and style. Frequent minor mechanical errors.

D: The essay presents a poorly-defined central idea and displays little insight. Ideas are not clear or developed. Introduction and conclusion are lacking or inadequate, and at times essay is hard to follow. Few stylistic techniques are incorporated. Numerous mechanical errors.

Finally, an easy, all-purpose form, such as the one below, could be used to evaluate any composition if students knew your expectations in each category. First formulate your objectives, then evaluate them. An example follows.

Assignment

Composition Evaluation					
	Poor	Fair	Good	Very Good	Superior
Form				✓	
Style					✓
Content				✓	
Mechanics				✓	
Overall effect					✓

Many times the author of a book will cite a particularly appropriate quotation which helps to illuminate the theme of the book. One such quotation for *Johnny Tremain* might be from John 12:24 in the New Testament, "'Truly, truly, I say to you, unless a grain of wheat falls into the earth and dies, it remains alone: but if it dies, it bears much fruit.'" How might this quotation help to illuminate one of the main themes of *Johnny Tremain?*

Resource: *Johnny Tremain Study Guide* by Gregory Power (Progeny Press)

Expectations for Each Category

Form: Introduction must include a "hook," something that captures the reader's attention and compels him to continue. Each paragraph must smoothly transition into the next.

Content: Must fully answer the assignment's question.

Style: Use action verbs. Do not use any forms of "to be."

Mechanics: Limit errors in areas previously taught.

Overall Effect: Produce a scholarly, but not stuffy, tone.

Although you probably would not take the time to write out specific expectations for each assignment, be sure to discuss them with your child so he understands what you expect. Once he masters a particular objective, transitions, for example, you could move on to new ones.

To Make the Writing Grade

You *can* make the writing grade. Follow your instincts. If something does not sound right, it probably is not right. Although you might not be able articulate the problem, you probably can fix it. By all means, use subjective evaluations, then learn writing techniques along with your children. For those particularly troublesome areas, enlist help. You might ask your child to give his assignment to three different adults, asking for constructive comments. Alternatively, you might profit from evaluation services, which are beginning to appear on the Internet.

Remember the writing maxims:

1. Understand the role of the five writing elements and set objectives in each area.

2. Evaluate students only on what they have been taught.

Above all, when teaching or evaluating writing, rest assured, *"Faithful is He who calls you, and He also will bring it to pass" (I Thess. 5:24).*

Chapter *15*
History Evaluations

In a broad sense we want our Christian children to see the hand of the Lord on the pages of history, to evaluate all events using the Bible as their standard, and to be able to apply the lessons learned to their own lives. We want them to understand:

He decreed statutes for Jacob and established the law in Israel, which he commanded our forefathers to teach their children, so the next generation would know them, even the children yet to be born, and they in turn would tell their children. Then they would put their trust in God and would not forget his deeds but would keep his commands (Psalm 78:5-7).

Some of the effects we hope will accompany our study of history will not be measurable. They are ideal, not quantifiable. For example, we cannot measure, "Inculcate a love of the Lord and appreciation for His sovereignty." We hope our child's faith increases as he studies. However, this internal change falls outside of our jurisdiction. It remains between the Holy Spirit and the child.

Some general objectives for history, which the student will be working toward his whole life, include:

1. Understand the broad sections of time that make up history; for example, the Middle Ages, the Enlightenment, or the Reformation.
2. Memorize a framework of important dates on which to hang the chronology of history.
3. Identify the major historical figures as well as understand their basic character, religion, and political views.
4. Understand the prevailing thought of the day in terms of philosophy, world view, religious presuppositions, or philosophies.
5. Grasp the major cultural features of the time including day-to-day activities, dress, food, dwellings, and days of celebration.
6. Be familiar with major wars and conflicts as well as their causes.
7. Identify inventions, such as the printing press, and their impact.
8. Study the history of the church and progress of the gospel.
9. Recognize the geographical features and the impact of geography on the cultures studied.
10. Evaluate the nations and kingdoms of the past in terms of their obedience or disobedience to God's Word.

Just how are these objectives to be evaluated? In history courses a number of options exist. Some of the more prominent include using

Tests	Reports
Assignments	Projects
Research	Reading
Note-Taking	Discussion

Since we have already discussed tests and discussions (see Chapters Six and Eight) we will not review them here. Instead we will explore the role of research, projects, reports, and reading with respect to history evaluations.

A Mentor Mom Shares
HOW WE MADE THE GRADE

"I use essay exams a lot in history and biology. I'm looking for specific content. I use a grid, a list of what I'm looking for which says students get one point if they mention this concept and one point if they mention that concept, this idea, this vocabulary term. Those are prewritten. In history students have to have a thesis statement, three major ideas that of course answer the question, then at least two supporting facts under each major idea. Almost all the grades this year have been from in-class essays."

✒Research

With the advent of relativism and the historical revision we see in our time, we need to teach our children to research so they can find, recognize, and know truth. Although younger students can research using resources from the library, older students should learn to find and use primary sources, those written close to the time period being studied. Examples of primary sources include letters, journals, diaries, articles, autobiographies, and sometimes books.

You might quantify research criteria by specifying how many references you want your child to find. A younger student might locate one library reference and obtain a number of quotes (three for an A, two for a B, and one for a C, for example). An older student might be required to find [three] primary sources with at least

[five] quotes from each. Depending on your intent, you determine the exact number of sources and quotes.

A number of resources other than primary and secondary books exist. Students learning to research might use the Internet, periodical archives, library databases, microfiche, census records, newspapers, local history archives, rare book rooms, and used-book stores, as well as the many other references available at libraries. To quantify research criteria, list the number required for each evaluation.

In another way to evaluate, design research exercises. For example, at the entrance to the library ask your child:

> "Whose 1954 Pulitzer Prize winning autobiography was entitled *The Spirit of St. Louis?*"
>
> (Question from *Information, Please! Advanced Level* page 17)

Give your child a specified amount of time, say ten or fifteen minutes, to locate the answer. Repeat this exercise on several occasions, then evaluate by his response time or, alternatively, how much his response time improves.

✒Note-Taking

Along with research, students need to learn to take notes. Although applicable to almost all courses, note-taking is especially useful in history. How should you evaluate your student's notes?

At least three possibilities exist. First, the student could receive credit if he took notes at all, or on some sort of scale such as this:

C: Student took at least one note.
B: Student took at least a page of notes.
A: Student took at least two pages of notes.

Alternatively, the quality of the student's notes could be evaluated:

C: Student's notes included all major headings.
B: Student's notes included all minor headings.
A: Student's notes included all important details.

In a final way to evaluate notes, allow a few days or a week to pass, then administer an open-note quiz. Allow your student to answer questions, orally or in writing, using his notes. Evaluate the result objectively, as you would a test.

✒Reports

Teachers evaluate most history reports (as well as science reports) in terms of content. Sometimes, teachers award two separate grades, one for content and another for mechanics (see Chapter 14, "Writing—Evaluating Compositions"). To properly evaluate, take care to articulate a specific assignment. For example, "Write a report about the White House" is too vague. How long should it be? Can it be on any White House topic including architecture, interior design, or construction, or should it only concern people, such as presidents, first ladies, or presidential children? Will sources be required in a bibliography? If so, how many? Unless you spell out your expectations, your child will not know how to meet them.

The best question will let your student know exactly what you require and how you will evaluate his answer:

✳ Write a type-written and double-spaced report on some aspect of state history. You might choose a biography of some important person or a description of a specific place such as a mission, military fort, or historical site. The report should contain a minimum of three topics; for example, the person's three contributions or three uses of the historical site. Include a bibliography which references more than one source, and a minimum of one quote from one of these sources, as well as an introduction and conclusion. Mechanical errors should be minimal.

Such a specific assignment simplifies grading. The following evaluation could be used:

C: Report meets but does not exceed the requirements.
B: Report exceeds requirements.
A: Report significantly exceeds what was asked.

Alternatively, tailored grading criteria for this assignment could be delineated:

C: Report contains an introduction and conclusion, contains three topics, one quote, and more than five mechanical errors (grammar or punctuation). Bibliography contains two sources.
B: Report contains an adequate introduction and conclusion, four topics, two quotes, and between three and five mechanical errors. Bibliography contains three sources.
A: Report contains an interesting introduction and conclusion which draws reader into the subject, five or more topics, two or more quotes, and two mechanical errors or less. Bibliography contains four or more sources.

As we discussed in the previous chapters, take care when combining criteria. We will note a problem if we record the criteria in a table, which appears at the top of the first column on the following page.

Criteria:	C	B	A
Introduction	present	adequate	interesting
Topics	3	4	5 or more
Quotes	1	2	3 or more
Mechanical errors	5 or more	3-5	2 or less
Bibliography sources	2	3	4 or more

What do you do if all the requirements for the A were met except for the number of quotes? If your student writes a report with an interesting introduction, five subtopics, one mechanical error, five bibliography sources, but only one quote, what grade should you award? There are two alternatives. First, design a rubric, assign a numeric value to each of the criteria, and compute an average. For example the student could earn fours (A's) for all of the criteria except the quotes, which could earn a two (C). His average score would be 3.6 $(4 + 4 + 4 + 4 + 2 = 18 \div 4 = 3.6)$. If your grading scale considered 90 to 100 percent to be an A, the report would earn an A $(3.6 \div 4 = 90\%)$.

Alternatively, if you required all of the criteria in a given grade category to be earned, the report would earn a C because of the lack of quotes. If you use multiple criteria, you also need to decide how they will contribute to the grade.

Although content is usually the primary evaluation tool for history reports, other means exist. You might evaluate the process of writing the report. This method works especially well for the first several reports your children write as they strive to learn the procedure. Evaluate various steps, such as choosing or narrowing the topic, research, notes or note-card preparation, report format (introduction, topics, and conclusion), drafts, and final product. You could evaluate each step subjectively based on how well your children performed, or objectively. An example of objective criteria for note cards might include the number desired (in total or for each topic), or how well the student followed the format you specified for note-cards (such as title, source, page number, and note). For more information on this topic, see Chapter 13, "Writing—Evaluating the Process."

ᔥProjects

A project consists of some sort of visual presentation of the points learned in a history lesson, for example, a model of a historical site, a display board showing a state's points of interest, a costume, or a relief or salt-dough map. Although unique, all projects can be evaluated according to certain characteristics:

Presentation—The presentation shows thought and creativity. The viewer wants to look closer and feels invited to linger. Any titles, graphics, illustrations, maps, and captions work together. Student delivers oral presentation with poise and confidence.

Organization—Thought, time, and care went into the organization of this project. Details fit within the overall theme. Content is easy to follow.

Accuracy—Material is accurate and error free.

Content—The project shows a thorough knowledge of the subject. An oral presentation is lively, informative, or thought-provoking.

As always, you have the option of evaluating the project subjectively based on how well your student performed the assignment.

C: Project meets but does not exceed the requirements.

B: Project exceeds requirements.

A: Project significantly exceeds what was asked.

Alternatively, you might combine the above project evaluation criteria in several ways. First, rate each area with the numeric equivalent of a grade, from four for an A or superior, to a zero for F or fail, then average the four numbers:

Area	Numeric Grade
Presentation	A (4)
Organization	A (4)
Accuracy	B (3)
Content	B (3)
Total	$14 \div 4 = 3.5 = B$

Second, give each criteria a weight to indicate its relative importance:

Area	Numeric Grade	Weight	Total
Presentation	A (4)	10%	.4
Organization	A (4)	10%	.4
Accuracy	B (3)	20%	.6
Content	B (3)	60%	1.8
Total			3.2 = B-

Finally, if you use projects frequently, you could create a generic chart and assign points:

Circle number of points for each area:				
Presentation	1	2	3	④
Organization	1	2	3	④
Accuracy	1	2	③	4
Content	1	2	③	4
A (90%): 15-16 B (80%): 13-14 C (70%): 11-12				

All of these methods yield essentially the same information but slightly different grades. Choose the easiest method that meets your objectives or purpose.

✎Reading

Students easily learn about history by reading. In fact, one educational philosophy, sometimes called the living book approach, advocates reading almost exclusively. In the absence of any other assignments, how can you evaluate your student and determine whether or not he achieves course objectives?

A nineteenth-century educator named Charlotte Mason advocated a variation of the living book approach as well as an evaluation method called *narration*. (Miss Mason also advocated other uses for narration which, unfortunately, exceed the scope of our topic.) In the appendix to volume 3 of her Original Home Schooling Series entitled *School Education*, Miss Mason gives examples of students' narration from end-of-term exams. She also offers some commentary which might be used to evaluate them:

"One notices the verve with which the children tell the tale, the orderly sequence of events, the correctness and fullness of detail, the accuracy of names." (p. 276)

"I think the reader will observe that due growth has taken place in the minds of the girls, both as regards judgment and power of appreciation." (p. 294)

Evaluation of Miss Mason's objectives (she called them objects) and evaluation criteria could be summarized:

Historical Fiction Evaluation				
	Poor	Good	Very Good	Superior
Verve (enthusiasm/energy)				✓
Order of events				✓
Fullness of detail			✓	
Accuracy of names			✓	
Judgment and appreciation		✓		

Evaluation of each category above would be subjective, of course, but an attempt has been made to quantify the subjective. The final grade could be computed as an average of the five objects (3.2 or very good) or as the minimum score (good).

If you do not want to evaluate each individual historical work, especially if your goal was exposure only, use the point system. The student earns his grade depending on the number of books he reads: A: Read

[10] books on the subject, B: Read [8], C: Read [6], D: Read [4], F: Less than [4]

Finally if you had the time, you could use a variation of the mastery approach. If, through some sort of evaluation such as narration, discussion, a test, or a book report, you find your student did not grasp the subject, assign more living books. Repeat until he achieves the desired understanding. At that point award an A.

A Mentor Mom Shares

HOW WE MADE THE GRADE

"My history criteria was really simple. In history my children did a family history project, where they wrote about their family. If they did their work on the day they were supposed to, such as, 'Write a letter to one of your family members and find out something about them,' and then did something with the information they received back, then that was worth a certain number of points. We also used *God's World* magazine, and if they read from that a half hour twice a week, then that was more towards the grade. At the same time we were doing a mini-study of Denmark and England, because that's where my husband and my ancestors lived. So if they read out of books we got at the library, then all those things combined equaled an A.

"Instead of being more general about the subject, such as 'study family history,' I set specific goals. That helped because then I knew which part of the project most important. The family history was the most important, so I gave that 50 percent of the grade. But the Denmark and England study and *God's World* were only worth 25 percent each.

✎To Make the History Grade

In spite of problems, multiple criteria benefit history evaluations. I resisted using this method for some time. "Too much trouble," I thought. But, with more practice, I began to appreciate how well-thought-out criteria keep me from being arbitrary and keep me consistent.

On the other hand, they are difficult to formulate. With practice, you might find this technique useful. But do not feel inadequate if it takes you several tries to come to a system that works for you. In the meantime, more subjective criteria is fine.

Chapter 16
Science Evaluations

From anatomy to zoology and astronomy to oceanography, the subject of science offers many categories of fruitful study. Ideal aims for this area include seeing and appreciating the intricate creation as a revelation of its Creator. Students should understand

For since the creation of the world God's invisible qualities—his eternal power and divine nature—have been clearly seen, being understood from what has been made, so that men are without excuse (Romans 1:20).

Although we pray that our children will realize this ideal goal, measurable objectives for science courses generally fall into several categories:

1. Understand the Biblical basis for scientific endeavors, as well as the arguments for creation and evolution.
2. Learn information such as the names and characteristics of each kingdom, how many body parts an insect has, and the location of constellations in the heavens.
3. Conquer the language of science, including its nomenclature and vocabulary.
4. Use and apply mathematical principles, theorems, and formulas to scientific fields, such as converting Celsius to Fahrenheit or computing velocity.
5. Learn about the history of science and the men and women who made significant contributions to each field.
6. Work with laboratory equipment to repeat experiments in a controlled environment or conduct original research.
7. Participate in a variety of field investigations.
8. Present results of a scientific investigation in an accurate and inviting way, such as a display for a science fair, a notebook, or a report.

You can achieve part of objective one through Bible study using prepared resources or Bible study tools such as a concordance. To evaluate

* Look up verses and discuss them with your children. Test comprehension and retention with questions.
* Ask children to look up verses which pertain to the subject and record them in a notebook. Later ask them to explain how these verses apply to the scientific principle. The quality of their answers and/or the number of verses found could be used for measurement.

Many of these objectives might be measured by objective means, especially nomenclature, math formulas, and other factual information (objectives two, three, and four). You could use any number of means to measure progress, including written or oral testing, discussion, and reports. Since these means have been covered in other subject areas and in Chapters Six and Eight, we will refer the reader to those discussions. Additionally, much of the discussion in Chapter 15, "History Evaluations," regarding the evaluation of reports, applies to science as well.

Perhaps the most common way to learn about men and women in the scientific field, objective five, would be to read biographies. You could evaluate biographies with oral or written book reports, narration, or projects. Alternatively, these could be measured by quantity, something along the lines of three books for an A, two for a B, and one for a C. Again, much of the discussion in Chapter 15, "History Evaluations," on evaluating reading, applies to the area of science.

Measuring lab work, fieldwork, and presentations offers unique challenges for the subject of science. The remainder of our discussion will focus on these areas.

A Mentor Mom Shares
HOW WE MADE THE GRADE

"In science at the beginning of the quarter we did a unit on composting and ecology. We read from Janice VanCleave's book [*Ecology for Every Kid*] and my children did the experiments. They also started a compost pile. They read about composting and they watched a video and we tried it ourselves and it really didn't work because, I don't know, we couldn't get it right. Because they did the things I wanted them to do, because they did the experiments, because they did the reading, because they tried composting, they got an A in science.

"Then last quarter we did physiology and health and that was more reading. My children read together and asked each other the questions at the end of the chapter. There was no test."

ᕗExperiments—Lab Work

Objectives for labs and experiments vary from simple exposure to developing proficiency with equipment and research methods. Likewise, evaluations vary from simple to complex.

For example, you could design an experiment to illustrate the fact that water expands when frozen. Your child could partially fill a container with water, mark the level of the liquid, freeze it, and later note the subsequent level. If your purpose was to illustrate a scientific fact and make it understandable or memorable, your student would meet your purpose by completing the experiment. If complete, he would earn an A. If you wanted to include more factors, you could evaluate setup, cleanup, and procedural accuracy. Additionally, at some other time, ask your student to explain the scientific principle (e.g. water expands when frozen, or water molecules move more slowly at lower temperatures and the volume increases).

When experiments are a minor or supplemental part of science courses, you might prefer subjective measurement. However, if you use them as a major teaching vehicle, you might spend some time developing grading criteria to measure whether or not your student met his lab objectives. An example appears below, but remember, the categories should be based on your own course objectives.

Science Experiment Evaluation
Circle number of points earned in each category

	Poor	Fair	Good	Very Good	Superior
Procedures (All materials assembled, safety measures taken, instructions followed, appropriate setup and cleanup of work area.)	0	1	2	3	4
Accuracy (Student cared for equipment, accurately measured, followed instructions and obtained acceptable results.)	0	1	2	3	4
Understanding (Student demonstrated his understanding of illustrated scientific principles.)	0	1	2	3	4
Application (Student able to apply scientific principles to similar situations.)	0	1	2	3	4
Presentation (Experiment clearly and thoroughly presented in a report, project, display, discussion, or other method.)	0	1	2	3	4

Grading Scale— A (90-100%): 18-20, B (80-89%): 16-17
C (70-79%): 14-15
Less than 14 points: repeat the experiment

ᕗLab Reports

When your student approaches junior high and high school, you might ask him to conduct more involved experiments and record his conclusions in a lab report.

Lab Report Sections

Typically, a lab report contains the following sections:

* **Title** page
* **Purpose statement** indicating the question to answer. More involved lab reports might have a hypothesis.
* **Materials, equipment, and methods** listing the use of equipment and supplies. You could include observations, measurements, and results including tables, illustrations, and graphs. [Note, you might separate these sections for more involved labs.]
* **Discussion and conclusion** to record results, answer the question, or explain what was learned. If books were consulted they should be listed in a separate bibliography section.

Lab Report Evaluation

Each of these sections might be evaluated separately using subjective criteria (an evaluation of superior, very good, good, fair, or poor; then averaged), or with something more involved. Alternatively, a table could be used such as the one at the top of the next page.

If you wanted to spend more effort, you could develop tailored grading criteria to define levels of "complete," "clear," or "understandable." However, at some point you will experience diminishing marginal utility; that is, the amount of effort on your part does not justify the increase in clarity. (See discussion on the law of diminishing marginal utility in Chapter Nine.) On the other hand, some parents and students might benefit from highly-tailored criteria.

ᕗFieldwork

Fieldwork involves applying scientific principles to an actual project, usually associated with the outdoors, or making observations of all or some part of the creation. Examples include the following:

* gardening
* close examination of a habitat or part of a habitat, such as a 3 x 5-foot section of your backyard
* recreating the habitat of a creature for a short period of observation in captivity (e.g. watching a caterpillar spin or emerge from a chrysalis or a tadpole grow into a frog)

Lab Report Evaluation *Award five points for each section done correctly, zero for sections done incorrectly.*	Points
Title page: All required information is present (e.g. student's name, date of experiment, course title). Title accurately describes lab and catches the reader's attention.	
Purpose: Hypothesis, purpose, or question to be answered is understandable and clearly presented.	
Materials and equipment: Properly listed. Complete—no omissions.	
Procedures or methods: Understandable. Listed sequentially and easily followed. Good diagrams and interesting paragraphs with appropriate transitions.	
Observations: Complete and detailed. Show insight. Understandable.	
Error section: Record accuracy of instruments and description of events which influenced results.	
Data or measurements and results: Accurate. Clearly organized and recorded. Neat. Appropriate format used (illustration, graph, chart).	
Analysis: Show calculations needed to process raw data into useable form.	
Conclusion: Complete, clear, and understandable. Answers question. Verifies hypothesis or explains why hypothesis was incorrect. Accounts for success or failure of the experiment. Is interesting and enjoyable to read.	
Bibliography: Complete. Acceptable format.	

A = 45-50 B = 40 C = 35 D = 30 F = 25 or below

* manipulating environmental factors such as light, temperature, and moisture, then observing their effects
* observing weather patterns
* collecting specimens

The key to evaluating fieldwork, which is the key to evaluating all work, is clearly defined objectives. You need to ask yourself, "What is the intent of the fieldwork?" To illustrate how to evaluate scientific fieldwork, consider three examples: gardening, weather observation, and botanical collections.

1. Gardening

What objectives might you have for a gardening project? They might include these:
1. Test the soil to determine Ph, and either select plants which will thrive or change it.
2. Learn what plants grow well together and develop a plan for companion planting.
3. Build and maintain a compost pile.
4. Observe germination and draw representative sketches of each plant at weekly intervals.
5. Weed and mulch.
6. Determine and maintain proper watering and fertilizing schedules.
7. Research the Biblical principle of "first fruits."
8. Harvest and enjoy.

Gardening Evaluation

Well-defined objectives make evaluation of this gardening example fairly straight forward. Even so, you have a variety of options. The easiest would be to simply evaluate the outcome. After determining what kind of harvest should be produced, a garden which provided a superior harvest would earn an A, a very good harvest gets a B, and so forth. This criteria would work well, especially for a supplemental project.

Alternatively, you could separate the above objectives into two categories: those that must be done on a repetitive scale (watering, weeding, mulching, maintaining the compost pile, and fertilizing) and those which have some sort of visible output (the soil testing, drawings, research, planting plan, and harvest). Give your student credit for doing the repetitive work on a schedule and design criteria to evaluate the others.

2. Weather Observation

Another example might involve observing weather patterns. Objectives might include the following:
1. Each day observe weather patterns in the following areas:
   * cloud cover and type of formations
   * minimum and maximum temperatures
   * wind direction
   * barometric pressure
   * amount of precipitation
2. At the end of three weeks compile observations into neatly drawn charts, one chart for each area.
3. Write a short report describing how observations were made and assemble all into a booklet. Be sure to include a title page and cover.

Weather Observation Evaluation

The above objectives could be evaluated as follows:
1. Evaluate by number of observations student conducted without having to be reminded. Counts

for one third of grade. A: 14-15, B: 12-13, C: 10-11. If less than 10 observations were made, no credit will be given and the project must be repeated.

2. Rate charts, booklet cover, and title page subjectively as superior, very good, or good, taking into consideration neatness, accuracy, and completeness. Counts for one third of grade.

3. Grade the report subjectively as superior, very good, or good, according to the amount of detail student included to accurately describe his observation procedures. Counts for one third of grade.

3. Botanical Collection

As part of a biology course or botany unit, you might ask your student to collect and press plant specimens. Objectives could include these:

1. Collect a variety of botanical specimens. Do not collect in regional, state, or national parks, or on private property without permission. Specimens should include

   ✸ leaves with a variety of leaf margins, simple and compound leaves, and parallel, pinnate and palmate venation

   ✸ flowers—both monocots and dicots

   ✸ ferns and mosses

2. Press each specimen between several pages of newspaper and place under a stack of books. Check periodically and remove when dry.

3. Mount on card stock. Label with specimen name and classification, and date and place of collection. Slide into sheet protectors.

4. Display in an attractive booklet.

Botanical Collection Evaluation

You could employ many ways to evaluate this project:

   A: All goals met. At least [60] specimens displayed.
   B: All goals met. [50-59] specimens displayed.
   C: All goals met. [40-49] specimens displayed.
   Collection not complete until all goals are met.

Alternatively, specific quantities might be specified for each classification category.

   Oftentimes, you might choose to evaluate fieldwork subjectively, especially supplemental fieldwork. Even so, both you and your student will benefit and stay focused when you take the time to quantify some of your subjective criteria.

❧Science Projects

At some point in their academic career, most students will enter a science fair or complete a science project. Usually the project consists of a question to be answered (for example, "Which brand of popcorn yields the smallest number of unpopped kernels?"), an experiment to answer the question, a display showing the results, and an oral presentation to explain these results to a judge. Usually judges evaluate each of these categories separately. Using the pre-printed form shown in Appendix C, Chart 2, you can make an evaluation form like the one below.

Science Fair Evaluation *Circle number of points*					
Hypothesis (Question clearly explained, displays originality and creativity)	1	2	3	4	5
Procedure & results (Sequence understood, explanation clear)	1	2	3	4	5
Conclusion (Scientific principles understood, accurate, appropriate research conducted)	1	2	3	4	5
Display (Neat, attractive, clear, thorough, and easy to understand)	1	2	3	4	5
Oral presentation (Clearly explained to judge, student exhibited poise and confidence)	1	2	3	4	5
Total Points: _____ A = 23-25, B = 20-22, C = 17-19, D = 15-16, F = below 15					

You could also use a simplified version of this evaluation form to grade a less-involved science project. For example, if you asked your student to assemble a mammal poster using pictures cut from old magazines, you could evaluate it subjectively in terms of accuracy of content and quality of display.

❧To Make the Science Grade

No one course would use all of these evaluation techniques. In fact, some might use none at all. If you teach survey courses using textbooks, you might be more comfortable calculating objective grades using publisher-supplied tests. You might add some experiments, fieldwork, or projects as a course requirement but without specific evaluation. That is, the experiments must be performed, but not evaluated. If you prefer a hands-on or project approach you might want to experiment with some of the ideas presented in this chapter.

Chapter 17
Fine Arts Evaluations

Of all the subjects, with the possible exception of English, evaluating fine arts presents the greatest challenges to homeschool parents. Because of the postmodern training we received through our own schooling, as well as the media, we see fine arts as a personal expression of creativity. At first glance we think there is no way to objectively evaluate fine arts or even to quantify some of the more subjective elements.

However, as opposed to "expressing" themselves or "exercising their creativity," artists of the Renaissance period learned the basics of their art form by copying or imitating great works of the masters. They mastered artistic elements and techniques:

Art: line, line direction, shape, size, texture, color (hue, value, chroma), shadow and shading, perspective, design, pattern, and motion.

Music: blending of rhythm, melody, and harmony; music theory and vocabulary; instrumentation and its categories (woodwinds, percussion, brass, strings); dynamics, and expression.

In our postmodern era, we believe these elements no longer matter. Without benefit of preliminary training in the basics of the art form, we expect our students to bring forth innovative designs and compelling works of art. No criteria exists for evaluation. One person's "good" might be another person's "awful."

However, since God has given us a standard for fine arts in His Word (see *Bible Truths for School Subjects* by Ruth Haycock), as Christians we cannot hold to this unbiblical philosophy. Instead, we must evaluate fine arts from His perspective.

Finally, brothers, whatever is true, whatever is noble, whatever is right, whatever is pure, whatever is lovely, whatever is admirable—if anything is excellent or praiseworthy—think about such things (Phil. 4:8).

If we were to summarize God's purposes for art, we could say it should do the following:

1. Edify, that is, build up the body of Christ.
2. Communicate Biblical truth through a variety of means including symbols, allegories, and types.
3. Point the audience to the Lord.
4. Be enjoyable. Above all, art should be recognized for its glory and beauty.
5. Exhibit technical skill and fine craftsmanship.
6. Improve the audience.

To illustrate how these purposes apply to fine arts and how teachers evaluate them, we will consider two areas, applied art and art appreciation.

ᴥApplied Art

Applied art means learning or becoming proficient in an art form such as painting, sculpting, playing a musical instrument, or composing. This entails three areas.

Principles

In contrast to the postmodern premise, students cannot become proficient in any art form until they master its basics, rudiments, or principles. For example, to learn to play the piano students must learn music theory, the location of each note on the keyboard, and fingering patterns. They also learn that *forte* means loud and *pianissimo* means very soft. If they were learning to draw, they would learn how to use perspective and shading.

Practice

Practice involves exercising those principles on a regular basis to improve skill and hand-eye coordination. The piano player's eyes, brain, and nerves must be trained to translate a musical score into signals sent through fingers to produce a musical pattern. The artist learns to hold his pencil and how much pressure to apply for a desired line.

Expression

It is possible to understand the nomenclature of a piece and play all of the notes correctly with perfect timing, but still have a dull and lifeless presentation. Additionally, it is possible to understand the principles of drawing, yet produce a sterile and tedious work. Expression involves putting knowledge and skill together to produce music with an emotional response or an inspiring or thought-provoking drawing. Expression gives art life.

Many times we only evaluate the final product of art, such as the drawing or the piano performance. However, since each art form entails three separate but inter-related steps, it might make sense to evaluate each of these separately. The question becomes, how?

Evaluating Principles

Art principles and rudiments can be evaluated objectively. Each note on the keyboard has a particular name. The color wheel has a definite structure. Particular brushes are more useful for some tasks than others. Paints should be mixed according to directions. In evaluation you could use any of the objective means we have previously discussed. To evaluate music principles, use checkups, tests, and quizzes included in some music theory and art instruction books. Alternatively, you could quiz orally. Test your piano student while he is seated at a keyboard. ("Tell me what this key signature means. Which of these notes is a whole note? How many beats does it get in this measure?") Quiz your child while he looks at a particular painting. ("How has the artist used principles of light in this painting? From what direction is the light source? What is the painting's focal point?")

Evaluating Practice

You might gauge practice quantifiably. Since your student obtains proficiency with frequent practice, create some sort of practice scale. For example, your piano student might need 150 hours of practice over a year for an A, 130 for a B, and so on. Alternatively, since piano practice should also be consistent, the scale could include a daily goal of, perhaps, 30 or 45 minutes of practice. If over a ten-day period, the student missed 0 to 1 days he would earn an A, two days for a B, three days for a C, and so forth. Likewise, the artist could be required to complete a certain number of sketches or exercises over the some time period.

A Mentor Mom Shares
HOW WE MADE THE GRADE

"Sometimes I ask my kids what grade they think they deserve. I have sat down with my son and asked, 'How are you doing in piano? Do you come to the piano every day without me having to remind you? Do you do it with a good attitude and for the full 30 minutes, rather than hopping up every ten minutes to see if you're done yet? That would be an A, to me that would be really excellent.' He smiles and says, 'Well, no.' Then I gave another example describing something really poor. He says, 'Well, no I don't do that either, I just do OK.' I say, 'Could you do better.' He'll say, 'Yes.' I've usually written out a grade that I think he deserves and he, for the most part, agrees."

Evaluating Expression

Most of us do not feel qualified to evaluate expression. In fact, most of us do not feel qualified to teach expression. Instead, we hire tutors to give our children music or art lessons. We can evaluate principles and

practice, but expression is beyond us. However, it should not be beyond our tutors. Consult with them to determine progress.

If you do evaluate expression, you will probably use subjective means. For example, after you teach your student certain principles, such as the difference between warm or cool colors, you could subjectively evaluate how color contributed to the mood of your student's painting. After you teach the difference between staccato and ritard, you could evaluate their use as your student plays a piece of music. Translate your evaluations, such as superior, very good, good, fair, and poor, into a letter grade.

Alternatively, if you possess talent and confidence and have an advanced student, you could find or compose a description of the final product and use it to subjectively evaluate your student. For example, the following describes criteria a piano adjudicator uses to judge an advanced student:

> Adjudicators will expect to hear the music performed at an appropriate tempo, one that matches the mood of the music but still allows the piece to sound technically under control. The judges will pay attention to the notes, rhythms, dynamics, touch distinctions, and use of the pedal, making certain that the performance matches the composer's intentions, as indicated in the score. They will listen for playing that is rhythmically stable, but not rigid. They will want the various musical ideas to be clearly differentiated and yet all belong together in a unified whole. They will expect the melodies to have a shape, but not bumps and lumps. (www.unm.edu/~loritaf/pnotperf.html)

Using the above narrative as the standard, you could subjectively rate the student on some scale such as superior, good, or needs improvement.

An easier subjective way to evaluate expression is to summarize it over the course of the evaluation period. For example, taking into consideration all of the principles taught, students could be evaluated as follows:

D: Expression stays the same
C: Demonstrates adequate improvement over the course of the semester
B: Demonstrates good improvement over the course of the semester.
A: Demonstrates superior improvement over the course of the semester

For students who exhibit talent in the arts and whose course of study emphasizes this area, you might benefit your student by taking the time to quantify expression

Advanced Piano Presentation				
4 = superior, 1 = needs improvement	1	2	3	4
Tempo (timing and rhythm matches music so it sounds technically under control)				
Technique (correct posture, finger skill, and movement of hands, arms and fingers)				
Accuracy (music played correctly, to match the composer's intention)				
Dynamics (musical notations followed, such as loudness, softness, staccato and ritard)				
Phrasing (breaks occur at appropriate intervals to separate into musical phrases, sentences or thoughts)				
Tone Color (chording, use of pedal, harmony, color, quality of sound produced)				
Expression (use of all the above elements so music is full of life and produces appropriate mood)				
Memory (music played without prompts or reference to score)				

criteria by listing and evaluating each element. By way of advantage, students will learn what elements they need to improve as well as those that sound fine. One of the reporting forms from Appendix C might be filled out with whatever criteria you use to evaluate expression. An example using Chart 2 from Appendix C appears above.

In another example, drawing objectives could be similarly quantified and might include the use of these techniques:

- ✳ **Color:** use of hue, intensity, and value
- ✳ **Shading:** use of cross-hatching, light, shadows, and contrast
- ✳ **Line:** use of texture, contour, angles, and curves
- ✳ **Perspective:** use of proportion, depth, vantage point, focal point, vanishing point and eye line
- ✳ **Composition:** use of positive and negative and horizontal and vertical space as well as contrast, harmony, and balance

Finally, performance goals for drama or voice could include areas such as energy and voice projection, diction and expression, pitch accuracy, tone quality, rhythm, poise, articulation, confidence, content, and style.

℘Art Appreciation

In contrast to applied art, art appreciation courses emphasize the history and elements of different art forms with a purpose of, well, appreciating them. Appreciation courses usually contain three areas.

Principles

Applied art principles and art appreciation principles are identical. However, instead of mastering them as will be required for the artist, an art appreciation student will benefit from exposure. By understanding the components the artist uses, your student will appreciate the skill and effort involved. A great ballerina makes the dance look effortless, something anyone could do. However, after learning all the ballerina had to master, your student will grow in his respect for the art form and the ballerina's talent.

History

Every art form has a history, usually with some sort of progression or school. Painting proceeds from Romanesque gothic in the 11th century to surrealism, abstract, pop and postmodern in the 20th. In addition to the art's history, during an art appreciation course a student should become acquainted with well-known artists such as Rembrandt and da Vinci or composers such as Vivaldi and Mozart.

Exposure

Exposure in an art appreciation course involves experience. After a student learns the principles of music, he should listen to a variety of composers and attend concerts, if possible. Upon studying schools of art as well as artists, he should examine reproductions from the library or perhaps visit an art gallery. Attendance at dramas, operas, ballets, and other performances provide exposure for appreciation courses in music and art.

Evaluating Principles

As discussed above, you can evaluate most art principles using objective criteria. Since the same comments under art courses apply to art appreciation courses, we will not repeat them here other than to observe that your standard will reflect exposure rather than mastery.

Evaluating History

In what by now might be a tired refrain, the key to evaluation is reachable, measurable, and specific objectives. Therefore, in order to evaluate the history portion of an art appreciation course, you need to delineate your objectives. An example follows.

Art Appreciation History Objectives

1. Using a concordance, student will research the field of art and list at least five Bible verses which explain God's perspective. Through discussion, student will learn how to apply God's standards to each art period.

2. Student will study ten periods of art history including Egyptian, Greek, Roman, Early Christian, the Renaissance, Baroque, Neo-Classical, the Pre-Raphaelites, Impressionism, and 20th century art. For each period student will:

   ✻ write a paragraph or two summarizing that style of art

   ✻ draw a sample of the art

   ✻ research two artists and write a paragraph or two comparing them

   ✻ draw artists' portraits or copy a sample of their work

   ✻ research the way the artists sign their work

   Assignment from *Feed My Sheep* by Barry Stebbing, and library resources.

Some students with little artistic ability or inadequate training might become frustrated with the drawing requirement. Consequently, you might ask for a diagram of the picture or a discussion of its design. Also, instead of drawing artists' portraits or samples of their work, your student could collect and display postcards.

You could set similar objectives for a music appreciation course. Time periods could include Greek, sacred or church music, baroque, classical, romantic, and modern. If you consult an encyclopedia or use prepared curriculum, you will be able to research the history of other art forms including drama and theater.

Once you set objectives, evaluation criteria should follow. Using the above example, criteria could be based on completeness and accuracy. Alternatively, you could take the time to list the elements each paragraph, drawing, or research assignment should include and evaluate your student's work against your list.

Evaluating Exposure

Since exposure in art appreciation courses involves encountering as many different works of art as possible, you might evaluate this area quantifiably. For example, a certain number of paintings might be examined or musical selections listened to for an A, something less for a B, and so on. Alternatively, if you combine several art forms, such as music and art, your student might be required to attend concerts and visit art galleries, or listen to recordings and view reproductions.

Although taking attitude into consideration might not be appropriate for all areas of study, it might be useful in evaluating art appreciation courses. If a student attends a concert with a closed mind or under some form of duress, he will receive little, if any, edification. Consequently, parents might find criteria, such as the following, very useful:

C: Student attended three concerts.

B: Student attended three concerts, was attentive and exhibited a willingness to learn.

A: Student attended three concerts, was attentive, and made a concerted effort to apply and understand concepts learned.

✺To Make the Fine Arts Grade

How detailed should you get when recording and calculating fine art grades? That depends entirely on your objectives, as well as your students' interests and talents. Some students who have a talent for fine arts might benefit from well-defined, quantified subjective grading criteria. Since these students will be practicing the art form over a long period of time, several years perhaps, it might be worth your time to think through explicit evaluation criteria to help your student achieve mastery.

For other students, including those participating for exposure only and those employing tutors, less-involved or more subjective criteria might be preferred. If, however, you have the time and inclination, any student will benefit from knowing exactly what is required from him and where he stands in relation to these objectives at any given time.

One final consideration for the "college prep" student. Some colleges require courses in the applied

> *A Mentor Mom Shares*
> ## HOW WE MADE THE GRADE
>
> "I use the mastery method in piano. Actually, I do not do it as much as the teacher does, but in the style my children are learning [Suzuki], they have to master the piece. They can't graduate until they have mastered it. It doesn't matter if they can hit all the right notes, it has to be perfect. That takes months. They'll spend a whole year in just one book. I knew when the piano teacher graduated my daughter from the first book, she had mastered it."

Chapter 18

Physical Education

The important area of physical education helps us to keep our bodies fit so we can serve the Lord. The guiding verse for this subject is

Do you not know that you are the temple of God and that the Spirit of God dwells in you? (I Corinthians 3:16).

Typically, physical education courses emphasize four areas:

1. Understanding the safety and participation rules for each physical activity as well as the systems used to produce movement (e.g. cardiorespiratory or muscular).
2. Promoting physical fitness to give strength and energy to serve the Lord.
3. Learning the skills necessary to participate in a variety of games, sports, and events.
4. Participating in all activities with a cheerful, willing heart. This includes learning to win and lose gracefully.

Evaluation methods will vary for each area.

❧Safety, Rules & Movement

Most objective testing methods serve to evaluate participation rules—how to score in tennis, the number of players needed to fill a volleyball team, or how many innings constitute a softball game. Written or oral tests could be used. Safety procedures could also be evaluated using any objective measure or by observation, because either they are obeyed or they are not. On the other hand, rather than evaluating them, you might insist that safety rules be followed at all times. If your children do not abide by them they cannot participate.

I once heard a story about tennis star Bjorn Borg. It seemed as a child he had a bad habit of throwing his racket when he didn't get his way or when he performed poorly. His mom put a stop to that. She took his racket away for a time and would not let him play tennis at all. If this story is true, good for her! Although he exhibited great talent and trained to become a professional, his mother thought more about safety (not to mention behavior) than talent.

In addition to safety and participation rules, this category also includes understanding the systems that produce movement such as the cardiorespiratory or muscle system. Although you can use objective means to evaluate them—how many chambers does the heart have or what is the name of the primary heart artery—

you could also use projects. For example, you might ask your child to keep a nutrition log or graph his pulse rate before and after exercising. You could evaluate using the point system, by number of times the activity is performed (such as 1 for C, 2 for a B or 3 for an A), or you might include the project as part of your minimum P.E. criteria and give full credit when the activity is complete.

❧Physical Fitness

There are two types of physical fitness exercises. In skill-related exercises, students train as athletes to perform a particular sport or skill. Components of skill-related exercises include agility, balance, coordination, power, and speed. The dancer might practice balance exercises, while the long distance runner might go for speed.

In health-related exercises the emphasis is on moderate but regular movement such as walking or everyday activities like yard work. Components of health-related exercise include cardiovascular fitness (walking, biking, jump roping, or swimming), body composition (which is the ratio of leanness to fatness), flexibility such as stretching exercises, and muscular strength and endurance achieved through activities like throwing, kicking,

---

A Mentor Mom Shares

HOW WE MADE THE GRADE

"People find it hard to grade P.E., especially in 4th to 5th grade. They'll think, 'Well, I've said go out and play. They've jumped rope a few times. I don't know, I guess I'll give them an A.'

"But it's also hard for other reasons. Let's say we're going to walk every day for 20 minutes as a family. Then, it's not my children's fault they didn't walk every day, it's my fault because I didn't get everyone up and out the door. My children can't go on walks by themselves. So then I can't give them a bad grade, because it's my responsibility. If I can't follow through on my responsibility, how can they follow through on theirs?"

or striking. The key to health-related exercise is that it must be performed consistently over a period of time.

For many homeschool families health-related fitness comes naturally. Active parents set an example for their children as they play a game of Frisbee in the park, take a hike in the hills, or go for a swim. Other families need to make a commitment to walk around the neighborhood, perform a stretching routine to an exercise video, or ride bikes. It should be easy to perform health-related exercises because, for the most part, they don't require a lot of equipment or special skills—just that commitment!

The point system works well to evaluate both health-related and skill-related fitness. You would need to ensure that your child performs the exercises safely and correctly, then have him keep track of how often he does them. When he reaches some predetermined point level, you award the appropriate grade.

ᔣAthletic Skills

The third area that normally comprises P.E. courses involves developing the skills necessary for athletic events or games such as batting for softball, ball delivery for bowling, or serving for volleyball. You have your choice of two different ways to grade these skills. Like writing and composition, you can choose to evaluate the product or the process.

Grading the product means focusing on the outcome such as sinking a certain number of baskets, achieving the next color belt, running a race in a certain time, and ultimately winning the game. Product evaluation might be useful and appropriate for children who show a talent in a particular area or who develop skills over several years. However, use caution. Even the best athletes have off-days or even "slumps." Baseball players who hit home runs also get thrown out. If you grade the product, you might find yourself in a situation where your talented child only earns the minimum grade.

When you grade the process, you avoid these potential problems because rather than performance you concentrate on skill technique and form like batting, running, fielding, and catching for softball. While product-oriented evaluation majors on how well or how far your child hit the ball, process-oriented evaluation looks at how well she performs each batting component—how she grips the bat, positions herself for the pitch, keeps her eye on the ball, swings and follows through, and drops the bat before running.

If you decide to evaluate the process rather than the product, the input rather than the output so to speak, keep a couple of things in mind. First of all, take into account your child's development level. A high school student can perform skills better than a first grader. Second, remember that skills develop with practice over a

long period of time. Your child will need plenty of practice before she is ready for evaluation. This goes along with the caution I have mentioned before: Never evaluate your child on something he or she has not been taught. Finally, remember that perfection is not a realistic goal. No athlete, even the elite professionals, consistently perform skills perfectly.

Another way to grade and evaluate P.E. skills does not use product or process. Instead, you can note improvement. As with grading the process, you will need to break down each skill to its component parts and evaluate them over some period of time. You would need to take notes to record a baseline, then chart improvement in each area like this:

Track Skills				
Skill	No Improve-ment	Some improve-ment	Good improve-ment	Great improve-ment
Stance—good hand and feet position		✓		
Start—no delays			✓	
Running—good arm and body form				✓
Finishing—follow-through and cool down			✓	

If your child is involved in some type of organized sport or takes a class like gymnastics or dance, you will probably rely on the instructor to evaluate your child. If you want to do it yourself but need help breaking P.E. skills into their component parts, I'd like to recommend a resource called *Dynamic Physical Education for Elementary School Children* by Robert P. Pangrazi (Pearson). Although oriented towards public schools, this book can be valuable for homeschoolers who are unfamiliar with the sphere of physical education. It tells how each sport is played, breaks each down into specific skills, offers a variety of fitness exercises, and illustrates all with pictures and diagrams. Plus, it offers many helpful suggestions on how to make rather than buy equipment—a consideration for homeschool families on a budget. The book is expensive, so look for a recent edition on a used book Web site like www.bookfinder.com. (**Note:** Not bookfinders!—a very bad site.)

ᔣBehavior

The final area you might want to look at when grading and evaluating P.E. is behavior. At the same time Bjorn Borg graced the tennis stage with his gentleman-like behavior, another tennis star, John McEnroe, provided a contrast. He also exhibited poor sportsmanship as a child, but his mother did not take away his tennis racket. She let the behavior continue. Years later, millions of spectators around the world got to witness her son throwing temper tantrums on the court. Not a pretty picture.

We want our children to exhibit Christ-like behavior at all times. We also want them to consider their fellow teammates as more important than winning the game. Competition has its place, but not when it tears another person down. Our children need to learn to play, win, and lose with grace.

Since Christ-like behavior should be the norm, rather than rewarding it you might take a negative approach. That is, you might lower the grade for a component performed with a bad attitude. Conversely, you might grade behavior positively, especially if this is something causing your child difficulty. You might increase a grade when your child exhibits good sportsmanship.

Finally, you might evaluate behavior separately from skill. Listing your criteria, like effort, attitude, or cooperation, you might grade each behavior using E-S-N, excellent, satisfactory, or needs improvement.

❧Putting it All Together

Your P.E. course could consist of all health-related fitness exercises, skills for one activity or more, or some combination of the two. You could also include a study of some body system or the rules of a sport or game. After your child has had ample practice, you could evaluate objectively, subjectively, or use a combination. Some examples follow.

Example One—Aerobic Exercise

If you seek to achieve aerobic fitness for your daughter, you might put together a course with the following aims:

1. Complete research to determine what the Bible says about physical fitness, especially how the body is the temple of the Holy Spirit.
2. Learn the effect aerobic exercise has on the muscular and circulation systems.
3. Perform some form of aerobic exercise for at least three times each week for at least 20 minutes each time. Student's heart rate should reach [some specified number] of beats per minute.

Objectives one and two could be evaluated with either objective or subjective criteria, while objective three could be quantified using some method such as Chart 1 to record how many times your daughter participated in the aerobics.

Although the charts may be useful to keep track of practices and exercises, they are not completely necessary. Alternatively, students could record their participation on a calendar, course log, lesson plans, or a monthly activity report. At the end of an evaluation period they could be totaled and the corresponding grade

calculated.

Example Two—Sport Survey

A few years ago a group of us homeschool moms pooled our talent and formed a P.E. co-op we called Home Team. Each month one of us taught the skills for a sport, put together a couple of pages of information from the Internet—rules, history, and techniques, and taught our children how to play. We chose sports our children were likely to encounter, that would use readily available equipment, and included bowling, kickball, ice skating, croquet, tennis, jump rope, volleyball, softball, and track. For each sport, we wanted our children to do the following:

1. Learn the rules as well as appropriate vocabulary and terms.
2. Properly care for equipment.
3. Understand the muscle systems needed to play the sport and how to exercise them safely, including warm up and cool down.
4. Perform fitness exercises at least three times each week.
5. Practice skills and play games or partial games weekly at our co-op class.

You could do the same for a sports survey course and evaluate each of the objectives differently. The first objective could be evaluated using a written or oral test, or by observing your child as he engages in the sport. Objectives two and three may be evaluated subjectively, by observation, as well. Objectives four, and five will need to be quantified. Chart 1 from Appendix C may be useful:

Sport Survey Course Record each date sport was practiced.					
Sport	Date	Date	Date	Date	Date
Bowling	9/7	9/14	9/21	9/28	
Kickball	10/5	10/12	10/19	10/28	
Ice Skating					
Croquet					
Tennis					
Jump Rope					
Volleyball					
Softball					
Track					

A similar chart could be constructed to record exercises.

The final decision for the sports survey course might be to determine how may practices of the sport or exercises would be required to earn an A, B, and C, and what weight each component would have. In one example:

- ✸ 10% know rules
- ✸ 10% care of equipment
- ✸ 30 % weekly exercise
- ✸ 50% sports practice

Objectives for this sports survey course concerned exposure only. In another course, perhaps one concentrating on fewer sports, you might require your student to reach some sort of proficiency. Examples include making a particular team in soccer, earning a certain rank in gymnastics or karate, or reaching a required status to participate in a competition, a particular level on the Presidential Fitness chart, or some other parent-defined criteria.

Example Three—Volleyball

In a final example, let's say you want your child to learn to play volleyball. You want him to be comfortable enough to join a group in a park or at a church picnic. You want your child to reach these ends:

1. Learn the rules of volleyball.
2. Learn to serve, bump, and pass.
3. Comfortably participate in volleyball games.

For objective one, you could evaluate objectively with a written or oral test. Objective three should be evaluated subjectively and for objective two, you might evaluate each skill component like this:

Volleyball Bumping Skills			
Skill	Fair	Good	Excellent
Move under the ball. Keep eyes on it.	✓		
Maintain proper stance and arm position			✓
Lift with entire body, not just arms.		✓	
Follow through.		✓	

A Mentor Mom Shares
HOW WE MADE THE GRADE

"My son took karate lessons for many years from a Christian dojo [karate school]. The instructors formed a plan for each student, estimating his progress and when he would be likely to test for the next belt. I based his grade on his commitment to practice, how well he matched his instructor's estimates, and other input from the instructor.

"My daughter isn't involved in any sport or organized activity other than Scottish Country dance which only meets once a week. While part of her grade is based on her commitment to practice, attend classes, and participate in Scottish Country dance demonstrations and adjudications, it's not enough to complete the 150 hours I require for the course. So, for the rest of the grade I count hours. If she exercises for 45 hours each semester she receives a C, 50 hours any time during the semester is a B, and 50 hours evenly spread throughout the semester, that's an A."

✑To Make the P.E. Grade

So often we give automatic A's when we grade P.E. Perhaps we are worn out by all the effort we spend thinking through evaluation criteria for other subjects. When we get to P.E., we give up. Hang in there! With a bit more effort, even P.E. courses may be equally evaluated.

Chapter 19
Wrapping It Up

We have come a long way. We have learned much about how to apply various grading methods to each subject. Before concluding, I would like to back up and reiterate something I said before.

When I was much younger, about eighteen or so, my father had this annoying habit of telling me something three times. (Now that I have raised eighteen-year-olds myself, I understand why!) I would argue that since he already told me whatever it was we were discussing, there was no need to do so again (and again). My dad maintained that in order for someone to truly hear what you have to say, you must repeat it at least three times. I have my doubts, but just in case my father was right:

This book contains suggestions. One of the major benefits of homeschooling is the ability to design your course of study so that it reflects your family's personal philosophy of education. Grading measures and states how well your student met the goals, plans, and objectives you set for the course. Some of the suggestions here will not fit in with your philosophy. Leave them. Others will work well. Use them. Some will spark other creative ideas of your own. Adapt them. Above all, remember the Lord's admonition to the Galatians.

Stand fast therefore in the liberty wherewith Christ hath made us free, and be not entangled again with the yoke of bondage (Gal. 5:1).

✆A Prayer for You

Most gracious heavenly Father, I pray that the people reading this book would find freedom in You. I pray that they would seek Your will for their children and their families as they raise the children You have given them. Lord, we have these precious gifts for such a short time. Teach us so we can teach our children. Guide parents so they can guide their lambs. Lead them so their children can lead the world. Help parents to take the ideas in this book and use them for Your glory and honor. We ask for wisdom.

In Your most precious Name,
Amen

A Mentor Mom Shares
HOW WE MADE THE GRADE

"I would encourage parents to be confident in themselves. The Lord has chosen you to be your child's teacher. We do tend to compare ourselves with all those others out there, and sometimes I don't know if they even exist, those perfect ones. We need to have confidence in what we're doing. We need to have integrity and not just arbitrarily give our kids grades, but we also need to have confidence that what we're doing is right. I love my kids. I wouldn't give them anything just to get them through, because I want the best for them."

Standard Grading Definitions

A - Superior. Work reflects a level of accomplishment significantly above the minimum.
Excellent, first rate, of the highest order, very remarkable, extraordinary, marvelous, wonderful, splendid, standout, outstanding, striking, supreme, the best, first-class, prime, admirable, noteworthy

B - Above average. The student has done more than just complete the assignments or course work.
Very good, fine, quality, choice, solid, precise, accurate, detailed, careful, meticulous, particular, worthy, meritorious, estimable, praiseworthy, competent, commendable

C - Average. Work meets, but does not exceed, the requirements.
Good, satisfactory, acceptable, serviceable, presentable, admissible, medium, good enough, passable, up to par, tolerable, permissible, allowable, all right, suitable, fair, no great shakes, middling, minimum, lowest acceptable, adequate

D - Below average. Work is inadequate.
Insufficient, too little, not enough, wanting, mediocre, inferior, below par, unsatisfactory, disappointing, unsuitable, flawed, faulty, deficient, lacking, meager, scanty, marginal

F - Fail. Work fell significantly short of the requirements.
Poor, failing, not acceptable, not passing

Common Grading Scales

Six popular models define letter grades based on the percentage of questions answered correctly. The percentage is determined by dividing the number correct by the number possible and multiplying by 100. For example:

Total number of questions: 80
Number student answered correctly: 72
Percentage: 72 / 80 = .90 x 100 = 90%

Scale One:	Scale Two:	Scale Three:	Scale Four:		Scale Five:		Scale Six:	
A: 90-100%	A: 93-100%	A: 93-100%	A	95-100%	A	96-100%	A	96-100%
B: 80-89%	B: 86-92%	B: 85-92%	A-	90-94%	A-	93-95%	A-	93-95%
C: 70-79%	C: 77-85%	C: 75-84%	B+	87-89%	B+	91-92%	B+	91-92%
D: 60-69%	D: 70-76%	D: 70-74%	B	83-86%	B	88-90%	B	87-90%
F: Below 60%	F: Below 70%	F: Below 70%	B-	80-82%	B-	86-87%	B-	85-86%
			C+	77-79%	C+	83-85%	C+	82-84%
			C	73-76%	C	80-82%	C	78-81%
			C-	70-72%	C-	77-79%	C+	75-77%
			D+	67-69%	D+	75-76%	D+	73-74%
			D	63-66%	D	72-74%	D	71-72%
			D-	60-62%	D-	71-70%	D-	70%
			F	Below 60%		Below 70%		Below 70%

Note: Most homeschoolers use scale one, especially those who are college-bound. Because most colleges consider it the standard grading scale, students may be at a disadvantage if they use another. If you use a different scale, make sure you indicate it on your high school transcript.

Appendix B
Addresses

The phone numbers and Web addresses of all available products mentioned in Making the Grade *are listed below.*

Teaching Materials

Bible Truths for School Subjects by Ruth Haycock, from Association for Christian Schools International (ACSI), (800) 367-0798 or www.acsi.org

Biology—God's Living Creation from A Beka Book, (877) 223-5226 or www.abeka.com

Christian Home Educators Curriculum Manual Elementary Grades and *Junior/Senior High* by Cathy Duffy, Grove Publishing, (714) 841-1220 or http://www.cathyduffyreviews.com

Ecology for Every Kid by Janice VanCleave, Wiley Publishing at www.wiley.com

Evaluating for Excellence by Teresa Moon. Available from many resource providers; just Google the title and author.

Feed My Sheep by Barry Stebbings, (800) 982-DRAW (3729) or www.howgreatthouart.com

Format Writing by Frode Jensen. Available from many resource providers; just Google the title and author.

Elements of Literature, Fundamentals of Literature from Bob Jones University Press, (800) 845-5731 or www.bjup.com

G.A. Henty Series from Preston Speed Press, (570) 726-7844 or www.prestonspeed.com

Gods and Generals by Jeff Shaara, www.amazon.com

God's World Magazine from God's World Publications, Inc. (704) 253-8063 or www.gwnews.com

High School Handbook by Mary Schofield, CHEA of California, (800) 564-CHEA or www.CHEAofCa.org

Information, Please! D.P. & K. Productions, available from many sources. Just Google the title and publisher.

Institute for Excellence in Writing by Andrew Pudewa, (800) 856-5815 or www.writing-edu.com

Killer Angels by Michael Shaara, www.amazon.com

The Kingdom of God from Christian Schools International, (800) 635-8288 or www.csionline.org.

The Last Full Measure by Jeff Shaara, www.amazon.com

The Light and the Glory and *From Sea to Shining Sea* by Peter Marshall and David Manuel, www.amazon.com or numerous resource providers.

Progeny Press Study Guides (Literature Study Guides),

(877) 776-4369 or www.progenypress.com

Saxon Publishers, (800) 284-7019 or www.saxonpub.com

School Education by Charlotte Mason (Book three of *The Original Home Schooling Series*) available from www.amazon.com

Science and the Bible by Henry Morris (Institute for Creation Research), www.icr.org

Senior High: A Home-Designed Form+U+La, by Barbara Shelton, Homeschool Seminars & Publications, (360) 577-1245 or www.homeschooloasis.com

Show Me Thy Ways by Gertrude Hoeskma (Reformed Free Press), (616) 224-1518 or www.rfpa.org

Stop Setting Goals by Bobb Biehl, (800) 443-1976 or www.masterplanning.tv or www.amazon.com

Streams of Civilization by Christian Liberty Press, (847) 259-4444, and press 6 (credit card orders only) or www.class-homeschools.org

Test Builder CD-ROM from Bob Jones University Press, (800) 845-5731 or www.bjup.com

Total Language Plus, Inc. (Literature Study Guides), (360) 754-3660 or ww2.integrityol.com/tlp

United States History from A Beka Book, (877) 223-5226 or www.abeka.com

What Your Child Needs to Know When by Robin Scarlotta, Heart of Wisdom Publishing, or www.heartofwisdom.com

Wordsmith Craftsman by Jeanie Cheney. Available from many resource providers; just Google the title.

World History (videos) by Linwood Thompson (The Teaching Company), (800) 832-2412 or www.teach12.com

The Write Source Series, Great Source Education Group, (800) 289-4490 or www.greatsource.com

The College Board

For information on the Advanced Placement and CLEP tests, call (609) 771-7243 or go to www.collegeboard.com, (45 Columbus Avenue; New York, New York 10023).

Appendix C
Chart 1

Course: _____

Student: _____   Credits: _____

Grade: _____   Date: _____

Appendix C

Chart 2

Course: ______________________________

Student: __________________________________ Credits: ________

Grade: __________ Date: ________

Appendix D

Sample Course Description

Course Title: New Testament Survey   Subject: Bible   Grade: 6

Course Description and Objectives:

The purpose of this course is to become familiar with the New Testament with emphasis on the life of Jesus Christ. Through this study student should learn and appreciate the great sacrifice Christ made on her behalf. It is hoped her love for Him will grow. Specific course objectives:

1. Read the New Testament. At the conclusion of each chapter record date read on Bible reading checklist.
2. Memorize Luke 2:1-19, John 14:1-6, John 15:1-12, and Matthew 5:1-16.
3. Complete the 102 lessons in *Show Me Thy Ways* with accompanying discussions and assignments. The intent of the discussion questions will be to test student's comprehension of the lesson. The assignments will provide additional teaching, research and map work, and the opportunity to tests the student's application of the lesson to her own life.

Instructional Materials and Resources:

Title	*Author or Publisher*
The Bible, New King James Version	
Show Me Thy Ways	Gertrude Hoeksema, Reformed Free Publishing Association
Show Me Thy Ways assignment book	

Evaluation:

1. Bible Reading— 20 percent of grade.

To receive credit, student must log the chapter numbers and date read on the Bible Reading Checklist.

A: Student reads the 89 chapters of the New Testament by May 15.
B: Student requires up to one additional week to complete the reading.
C: Student requires up to two additional weeks to complete the reading.
D: Student completes the reading, but requires more than two additional weeks.
F: Student does not complete the reading.

2. Memorization—20 percent of grade.

An error consists of an incorrect recitation, a correction, or a requested prompt.

   A: no errors   C: two errors   F: more than three errors
   B: one error   D: three errors

3. Lessons—60 percent of grade consisting of equal parts discussion and assignments.

Discussion: Each lesson will contain at least one discussion question. At the end of the week student will be evaluated on how well she participated in that week's discussion:

C: Student is prepared for the discussion, having completed all assigned homework. With frequent prompting, questioning, and explanations, she can be led to an understanding of the concepts covered. She can appreciate and understand the insights and ideas of others.
B: Student is prepared for the discussion, having completed all assigned homework. She can be led to an understanding of the concepts covered through questioning. Occasionally, she will add her own insights and ideas.
A: Student approaches discussion prepared, with all homework completed and ready to participate. She shows understanding of the concepts covered and frequently adds her own ideas and insights. She volunteers thoughts pertinent to the subject.

Assignments: Additionally, once a week student will complete an exercise from the *Show Me Thy Ways* assignment book (map work, personal application, supplemental study, and retention testing). Each will be evaluated to see how well the assignment's objectives were met, and awarded a rating of "superior," "very good," or "good." Lessons with evaluations less than "good" will need to be repeated.

Bible Reading Checklist—Record chapter and date when reading is complete.

Chapter	Date	Chapter	Date	Chapter	Date	Chapter	Date	Chapter	Date	Chapter	Date	Chapter	Date	Chapter	Date

Bible Memorization

PASSAGE	DATE	ERRORS	GRADE
Luke 2:1-19			
John 14:1-6			
John 15:1-12			
Matthew 5:1-16			

Lessons & Discussion. Record letter grade for discussion and superior, very good, or good for assignment.

Week	Assign.	Discussion	Week	Assign.	Discussion	Week	Assign.	Discussion	Week	Assign.	Discussion
1			10			19			28		
2			11			20			29		
3			12			21			30		
4			13			22			31		
5			14			23			32		
6			15			24			33		
7			16			25			35		
8			17			26			35		
9			18			27			36		

Appendix D
Sample Course Description

Course Title: American Government   **Subject: Government**   **Grade: 11**

Course Description and Objectives:

This course will cover four areas:

1. **Biblical Perspective on Government**—Using the Bible, student will research the Biblical perspective on forms of civil government (self-government, decentralization, multiplication of sin, and spheres of government), the forms of God- and man-centered government, and the Biblical qualifications for leadership. Short papers (two or three pages) will be required to summarize and explain each.

2. **Election**—Beginning with the fall, student will follow the presidential election to its conclusion on Inaugural Day in January. Topics covered will include

    Primary: Student will learn about the two-party system, research the qualifications of the Republican candidates and build a profile for each, and write a short report on her experience at a convention she will attend where all the Republican candidates will be introduced,

    Campaign: Watch and analyze the candidates' acceptance speeches, follow weekly polls and graph results, review ballot issues to prepare for voting day, and write an essay on how the president is selected.

    Electoral College: Learn how it operates and, using an Internet model, predict which candidate will win in the electoral college using information from polls.

3. **Constitution**—Student will begin by reviewing the history of the Constitution and the occasion for its writing, and continue with in-depth study of each Article and Amendment. Student will complete exercises and assignments, participate in frequent discussions, and take periodic quizzes on material covered. Additionally, she will complete a poster illustrating the powers conferred by the U.S. Constitution and take a final Constitution test.

4. **State and Local Government**—Student will be introduced to the workings of government on the state and local level. She will complete assignments, participate in discussions, visit California's capitol and one senator or representative, and write one persuasive letter on some topic to an elected official.

Instructional Materials and Resources:

Title	*Author or Publisher*
God and Government (selections)	Gary DeMar
Our Living Constitution	Good Apple
Our Independence and the Constitution	Landmark
Teacher-supplied supplemental materials and notes	Internet

Grading Criteria:

20% Biblical Perspective: Average score of essays

40% Election: Average score of essays and projects

30% Constitution: Average of Constitution test score and Constitution poster. Note: student must obtain at least 80 percent on Constitution test. If a lower score is obtained student will be required to complete further study and take another test.

10% State and local government: Average score of projects

Additionally, student's grade will be increased or decreased one-half grade based on which description most closely applies:

Decrease—Assignments completed, but not on time. Answers display little effort or thought. With frequent prompting, questioning, and explanation, student can be led to an understanding of the concepts covered. Concepts not well-retained and require frequent review.

No change—Most assignments completed on time. Answers display average effort and thought. Student can be led to an understanding of the concepts covered through questioning. Moderate review required for retention.

Increase—Assignments completed on time. Answers show that student worked hard to think, look up, and determine correct answer. She took initiative in asking for help in problem areas as well as responsibility to retain explanations. With some prompting, questioning, and explanation student can be lead to an understanding of the concepts covered. Student takes responsibility for own review.

Appendix D
Sample Course Description

Course Title: Writing & Composition   **Subject: English**   **Grade: High School**

Course Description and Objectives:

The focus of this class is to learn to use structure and organization when writing reports and essays, as well as incorporating creative writing features. By analyzing and discussing selected works from *Elements of Literature* (BJUP), students will understand how authors use specific writing techniques. Then, students will learn to use the same techniques in their own writing. Eight essays will be required, each two to four pages in length, in the following areas:

Selection:	Essay Type:	Assignment:
The Fly by John Ruskin	Compare and contrast essay	Compare Ruskin's view of freedom to the Biblical. Look up John 8:32, 36; Rom. 6:18, 22 and 8:2; Gal. 5:1 and I Pet. 2:23-16. What world view does Ruskin hold to? Prove it with evidence from his essay.
The Spider and the Wasp by Alexander Petrunkevitch	Analysis	Petrunkevitch's essay is interesting reading. How does he accomplish this? Analyze his essay, identifying specific words or phrases that transform what could have been dull, scientific description into exciting narrative.
The Spider and the Wasp by Alexander Petrunkevitch	Expository	Choose a creature which interacts with another (predator/prey or symbiote/parasite, or beneficial such as butterfly/flower), and describe their relationship.
Pigeon Feathers by John Updike Plato: *The Parable of the Cave*	Literary analysis	Analyze how the characters illustrate the main world views: pantheist (romanticism), modernist (materialist), humanistic (self-autonomy), and Biblical. Describe the essence of the world view, then describe how the character illustrates it, giving specific examples from the story. In your conclusion, answer this question: From a Biblical perspective, what does Updike's story lack?
An Old-Fashioned Iowa Christmas by Paul Engle, and *A Miserable Merry Christmas* by Lincoln Steffens	Descriptive essay	Describe a Christmas past. Appeal to all the senses. Use techniques studied in the two Christmas passages. Ideas: tell about some unique family tradition or an unusual incident, or write from a child's perspective.
The Life of Caesar by Plutarch	Biography	Write a biography on some historical person. Rather than describing his life in general terms, narrow your focus to a few specific incidents that reveal his character. Include his spiritual status.
The Drummer Boy of Shiloh by Ray Bradbury	Literary analysis	Analyze Bradbury's story in terms of imaginative comparisons, symbol and theme. How do the imaginative comparisons and symbols contribute to the story's theme? Give specific examples.
On the Road Again with Recorded Books by O. B. Hardison, Jr., and *A Piece of Chalk* by G. K. Chesterton	Personal narrative	Write about a specific incident in your life. This might be a major turning point, a humorous anecdote, a time of great emotion, a revelation, fulfillment of a dream, or just everyday life. Make it interesting, incorporating literary techniques learned.

Course Title: Writing & Composition (cont.)

Resources Used Title	Author or Publisher	Type of Use (primary, reference, supplemental, specific chapters or pages)
Elements of Literature	Bob Jones University Press	Specific selections
Synonym Finder	Rodale	Reference
A Writer's Guide to Transitional Words and Expressions	Victor C. Pellegrino	Reference
The Gregg Reference Manual	William A. Sabin/Glencoe	Reference

Grading Standard

Each essay will be graded based on specific criteria in the following areas:
* form
* content
* style
* mechanics
* overall effectiveness.

Worth 50 points each (ten in each of the above areas), student may select the best seven out of eight essays for a total of 350 points.

    A: 315-350 points
    B: 280-314 points
    C: 245-279 points.

A total below 245 points is unacceptable and work must be repeated.

Appendix D
Sample Course Description

Course Title: American History   **Subject: History**   **Grade: 7**

Course Description and Objectives:

Student will study the progress of American history beginning with the Age of Exploration and continuing to the present era, paying particular attention to the problems and opportunities of each time period, major characters and their contributions, chronology of events, important terms and locations, and geography. Specifically:

- The Age of Exploration
- Colonial America
- War for Independence
- Jacksonian Era

- The War Between the States and Reconstruction
- The Gilded Age
- The World Wars
- The Modern Age

Student will:
1. Read all of *America, Land I Love* and take periodic tests.
2. Read up to four supplemental biographies from an approved list and write book reports on at least three.
3. Complete an in-depth project on some aspect of American history (teacher approval required) and participate in the local history fair.

Resources Used

Title	Author or Publisher	Type of Use (primary, reference, supplemental, specific chapters or pages)
America, Land I Love	A Beka	Primary
Biographies	From Approved List	Supplemental
Maps, Atlas, Encyclopedias		Supplemental

Grading Standard:

Tests—50 percent of grade
    Each test will be scored: A (93-100%), B (85-76%), C (75-70%), D (70-74%) F (below 70%)
    The best 10 out of 12 test scores will be used

Book Reports—20 percent of grade
    A: Three book reports submitted
    B: Two book reports submitted
    C: One book report submitted

Project—30 percent of grade
    The project will be worth a total of 100 points awarded as follows:
    Presentation   20 points
    Organization   20 points
    Accuracy   30 points
    Content   30 points
    A (90-100 points), B (80-89), C (70-79), D (60-69), F (below 60)

Evaluation Report

Student_____ Grade____ Qtr. or Sem._____ Year _____

Subject	*In each of the subjects listed below, evaluate your student in terms of your teaching objectives.*	
	Objectives Mastered (Areas of Strength)	**Continuing Objectives** (Areas in Progress)
Bible		
Mathematics		
Language Arts		
Science		
History/ Geography		
Fine Arts		
Health/Elective		
P.E. / Elective		

Appendix F - Report Card Example
School Name, Address, and Phone

Name: _____

Grade: _____ Date of Birth: _____ School Year: _____

Attendance	1st Qtr.	2nd Qtr.	3rd Qtr.	4th Qtr.	Total
Days Absent					
Days Ill					

Explanation of Grading Codes

A ----Outstanding   P ---- Pass
B ----Superior   N---- No Credit
C ----Good   I ---- Incomplete
D ----Fair
F ----Failing

Subject	1st Qtr.	2nd Qtr.	3rd Qtr.	4th Qtr.	Total
Bible					
Math					
English					
History					
Science					
Health					
Fine Arts					
P.E.					
Elective					

Comments

1st Quarter:
_____
_____
_____
_____

2nd Quarter:
_____
_____
_____

3rd Quarter:
_____
_____
_____
_____

4th Quarter:
_____
_____
_____
_____

Appendix F—Transcript Example

School Name, Address, and Phone

Student: _____   Parent: _____
Date of Birth: _____   Address: _____
Sex: _____   _____

9th Grade		1st Semester		2nd Semester	
Year:		Grade	Credits	Grade	Credits

Total Credits: _____
GPA: _____

11th Grade		1st Semester		2nd Semester	
Year:		Grade	Credits	Grade	Credits

Total Credits: _____
GPA: _____

10th Grade		1st Semester		2nd Semester	
Year:		Grade	Credits	Grade	Credits

Total Credits: _____
GPA: _____

12th Grade		1st Semester		2nd Semester	
Year:		Grade	Credits	Grade	Credits

Tests Scores, Honors and Awards:

_____
_____
_____
_____
_____
_____

Total Credits: _____   GPA: _____
Diploma Awarded: _____

Grading Scale: A: _____   B: _____
C: _____   D: _____

Date Printed: _____

_____
Registrar

Appendix G
How to Calculate a GPA

How to Determine Grade Point Average

1. Assign each course a value corresponding to the number of credits the course is worth. This will either be 1 for a year-long course and .5 for a semester course or 10 credits for a year's course and 5 for a semester.

2. Assign a numerical equivalent to each grade as follows (do not include P.E. courses):

Scale One:		Scale Two:	
A or A-	= 4	A	= 4.00
B+, B, or B-	= 3	A-	= 3.67
C+, C, or C-	= 2	B+	= 3.33
D+, D, or D-	= 1	B	= 3.00
		B-	= 2.67
		C+	= 2.33
		C	= 2.00
		C-	= 1.67
		D+	= 1.33
		D	= 1.00
		D-	= 0.67

> Add one to the numeric equivalent of an honors or Advanced Placement course. A grade of A– would be worth 4.67 in this example. (Note: some colleges award an additional .5 for honors courses, or 4.17 in this example.)

3. Multiply the numerical equivalent of each grade by the course value (credits).

4. Total the results of step 3.

5. Divide total points by the total course value (total credits). The resulting number is the student's GPA.

Example

Course	Grade	Year or Semester	Numeric Equivalent	Course Credits	Points
Bible	A	Year	4.00	10	4.00
AP (Honors) English	A-	Year	4.67	10	4.67
Algebra I	B-	Year	2.67	10	2.67
World History	B+	Year	3.33	10	3.00
Physical Science	B	Year	3.00	10	3.00
P.E.	A	Year	-*	-	-
Baroque Music	A	Semester	4.00	5	2.00
Industrial Arts	A	Semester	4.00	5	2.00
				60	21.34

GPA: 21.34 / 6 = 3.56

To calculate the GPA, multiply the numeric equivalent by the course credits to get the points. Divide the total points by the total credits. The result is the GPA.

*Please note that P.E. courses are usually not included when figuring the GPA.

Several GPA Calculators exist on the Internet that perform the mathematical calculations. To find one, type "GPA Calculator" into your favorite search engine.

ꙮSubject Index

Making the Grade

❧Scripture Index

.

61582589R00066

Made in the USA
Middletown, DE
12 January 2018